SPECIAL PRAISE FOR

400 Friends and No One to Call

"This book is a marvel! Without any pomposity, this is a compendium of real life stories and useful tips about solving the universal problem of loneliness. Val Walker is able to walk a fine line that never veers into 'clinical' distance or cloying sweetness. Instead she simply tells her own and her friends' stories with very helpful editorializing along the way. I plan to recommend this book widely!"

—**Jacqueline Olds, MD,** coauthor, *The Lonely American*, Associate Professor of Psychiatry, Harvard Medical School and Psychiatrist at Massachusetts General Hospital

"With honesty, compassion, and practical wisdom, *400 Friends and No One to Call* grapples with a critical and timely issue. At the Health Story Collaborative, we're thrilled to have Val Walker's knowledge and guidance for breaking through social isolation."

—**Annie Brewster, MD,** Massachusetts General Hospital, founder of the Health Story Collaborative and cofounder of The Opioid Project

"Perhaps now more than ever, the experience of loneliness and isolation is almost universal. In *400 Friends and No One to Call*, Val Walker brings a collection of diverse voices together to teach us how we can break past that isolation and build communities that support us and help us find our way. Her clear, empathetic, and compassionate voice carries the reader through the forces that isolate us and gives us tools needed to move to a new sense of belonging."

—**Allie Cashel,** president and cofounder of The Suffering the Silence Community, Inc., and the author of *Suffering the Silence: Chronic Lyme Disease in an Age of Denial*

"Human beings are deeply social animals who need each other for healing, comforting, and connection. In this vitally important book, Val Walker has given us an informative and heartfelt examination of a world that encourages the kind of isolation that will kill us if we allow it. Walker shows us the way out of the pain of isolation, offering wonderful insights about building connections and relationships that will sustain us when we need love, comforting, and healing. This book is a remarkable achievement and should be a must-read for all of us on this deeply challenging human journey."

—**Scott T. Allison, PhD,** author of *Heroes* and *Heroic Transformation*, Professor of Psychology, University of Richmond, editor of Heroism Science

"Val Walker has written an important book about a paradox of our time: We have friends all over the place, and yet no one to turn to in rough times—a paradox with serious ethical and social implications. Insight and hands-on advice are needed. For those who care, Ms. Walker's book is a must-read."

—**Claus Jarlov,** CEO, communications consultant, founder of Global Denmark, Copenhagen, Denmark

"The work I do in fighting the stigma and isolation of addiction is all about the power of community. We hurt as one and we must heal as one. *400 Friends* shows us how."

—**Paul E. Kandarian,** actor/writer, longtime contributor to the *Boston Globe* and *Rhode Island Monthly*

400 Friends

No One to Call

Val Walker

400 Friends
AND
NO ONE TO CALL

Breaking through Isolation
& Building Community

CENTRAL RECOVERY PRESS

Las Vegas

Central Recovery Press (CRP) is committed to publishing exceptional materials addressing addiction treatment, recovery, and behavioral healthcare topics.

For more information, visit www.centralrecoverypress.com.

Publisher: Central Recovery Press
             3321 N. Buffalo Drive
             Las Vegas, NV 89129

25 24 23 22 21 20   1 2 3 4 5

Library of Congress Cataloging-in-Publication Data

Names: Walker, Val, author.
Title: 400 friends and no one to call : breaking through isolation and
  building community / Val Walker.
Other titles: Four hundred friends and no one to call
Description: Las Vegas, NV : Central Recovery Press, 2020. | Includes
  bibliographical references.
Identifiers: LCCN 2019040437 (print) | LCCN 2019040438 (ebook) | ISBN
  9781949481242 (paperback) | ISBN 9781949481259 (epub)
Subjects: LCSH: Social isolation. | Loneliness. | Social networks.
Classification: LCC HM1131 .W35 2020 (print) | LCC HM1131 (ebook) | DDC
  302.5/45--dc23
LC record available at https://lccn.loc.gov/2019040437
LC ebook record available at https://lccn.loc.gov/2019040438

Photo of Val Walker by Barbara Olson.

Publisher's Note
This book contains general information about loneliness and social isolation, as well as the stigma of isolation and the shame people feel about lacking social support. Guidance for building community and friendship is offered, supported by social science research and related matters. The information contained herein is not medical advice. This book is not an alternative to medical advice from your doctor or other professional healthcare provider.

Our books represent the experiences and opinions of their authors only. Every effort has been made to ensure that events, institutions, and statistics presented in our books as facts are accurate and up-to-date. To protect their privacy, the names of some of the people, places, and institutions in this book may have been changed.

Cover design and interior by Marisa Jackson.

*This book is dedicated to what makes us brave enough
to break through isolation and reach out again.*

Table of Contents

Introduction

Once I Loved Being a Loner

It may seem strange that I would begin a book about healing from isolation by singing the praises of solitude. Long before I started writing this book, I once lived a cloistered, quiet life near a sanctuary of blue herons on the coast of Maine.

In 2000, at the end of a divorce, grieving that I was childless due to "premature ovarian failure" as the doctors called it, I moved to Maine with my cat to start my life all over again. I yearned to find my own "inner voice" after forty years of following the voices of others and craved the wilderness of the coast. I had fallen in love with the popular book *Women Who Run with the Wolves*, and indeed, I, too, was going to restore my soul by healing in the wild.

Four decades of people-pleasing and fake extroversion had overshadowed my introverted, highly sensitive nature to the point I could no longer recognize my own thoughts. Back in the 1960s in Virginia, wallflowers like me were raised to be effusive and gracious, no matter what, even if we looked utterly awkward at it. But, despite my lack of poise, my abundance of empathy, softheartedness, and idealism attracted lost souls who begged me to believe in their "potential"—and pulled me down to hell to save them. Miserable with myself for repeatedly being deceived and betrayed, I reached out to therapists in the 1980s who unfortunately knew little about the abusive tactics of narcissists or sociopaths. I was told that assertiveness, boundaries, and learning how to say no were all I needed to protect myself. Worn down from the constant violation of my boundaries, I blamed myself for failing at assertiveness and deemed I was too weak to stand up to bullies, both at home and at work.

It wasn't until I was in graduate school studying to be a counselor in the 1990s that I learned about the dynamics of abuse, bullying, and violence. I realized that it takes a supportive community to stand up to abuse and bullying and that no one can do this alone—no matter how strong or assertive we as individuals might be.

I cut ties with several people and places, but I still blamed myself for my failed relationships, even with my training in counseling. I longed for a good, clean break from being close to people. It was time to withdraw from intimacy and live like a nun, if not a mystic, in a pure, beautiful place where nature and my cat was all I needed.

For the first four years after I moved to Maine, I flourished in glorious solitude, practically living a monastic existence. I never felt lonely sitting on warm moss by the rocky, windswept coves near the blue herons at sunrise, watching their every move with utter reverence. I walked barefoot on the sandy banks of rivers alongside the herons as they waded at low tide and basked in the serenity of belonging in their private, watery worlds. The herons were my graceful guides to the joys of being fully present, freeing me from the fearful, cloying thoughts of my turbulent younger years. The herons taught me patience with their stillness and the fine art of timing, as they always knew exactly when to strike their prey. I softened in their presence and learned how to trust my instincts and ground myself. They showed me how to restore an authentic sense of grace at my core. Eventually, I learned the skills of mindfulness from long, peaceful hours spent in the wilderness alone with the herons, egrets, ospreys, geese, ducks, and other water birds.

My quiet life was well-balanced. I worked as a case manager for four days a week at a mental health agency, which allowed three days off to live my contemplative blue heron existence. I discovered that I could put the mindfulness learned from my quiet time with herons into practice at work while listening to the people I served as a counselor. I could stay still and enjoy a deeper sense of listening, a more patient, grounded, and unassuming sense of connection with my clients.

Ivan, my cat, and I spent tranquil times in my tiny studio apartment in an old sea captain's house by an apple orchard. Together we found joy in our shared little daily habits—giving him his shrimp treats while I cooked seafood pasta dishes, sniffing my cup of coffee with me when he jumped on my desk, trusting him to scope out my potted plants on the patio if he was good and didn't scamper off. On long winter nights, I curled up in a blanket with Ivan in my lap, reading, reflecting, and imagining books I might write. I filled journals with healing meditations from my long walks, which later became material for my first book, *The Art of Comforting*, a labor of love dedicated to the language of empathy and listening with open hearts and minds. During my ten idyllic years living in this quietude, I gradually managed to make three friends and enjoyed their families. I was invited to holiday dinners and rarely felt left out. When friends visited me, I served my seafood pasta meals at my table that could barely seat four. I cherished my simple and predictable life.

But by 2009, Maine suffered economic setbacks that affected my job in the social services field when funding was drastically cut for the Medicaid recipients I served. I couldn't find anything other than low-paying, part-time jobs, and I fell deeper into survival mode and despair. Ivan, my old cat buddy of seventeen years, died of kidney failure. By 2012, my best friend, Becky, had disappeared from my life without saying a word. Then, after my surgery, along with worsening chronic colitis and arthritis, my eleven-year-old car breaking down, and not being able to afford my rent, it was time to leave Maine for Boston.

Maine, as long as I could afford it, and as long as my health was good, had been my safe place where I trusted animals, herons, and the wilderness more than people. I had spent fourteen years of my life as a bit of a recluse, but now, approaching my sixties, I had to admit it: I needed people in my life.

Writing the Book I Couldn't Find

I've written the book I wish I'd had in 2012 when I found myself isolated with no one to call. It was startlingly clear that I needed to rebuild my social support networks, basically starting from scratch to find new friends and colleagues—doing a whole overhaul of my social safety net. Given such a daunting and intimidating task, I searched for a guidebook that was not only reassuring but would give me practical advice on rebuilding strong support networks. Amazingly, to my dismay, aside from some books about dating and hunting for partners, little was out there to help build support in isolating times. It seemed so obvious that many people in my situation needed help with lifelines to new friendships, fellowships, and communities. People recovering from isolating times such as illness, relocation, bereavement, or loss of a job certainly could use comforting yet practical guidance.

At first, not being able to find such a guidebook for people like me made me feel even more isolated. *Gosh,* I wondered, *are people supposed to face this long, lonely journey all by themselves? Or does our society just assume we all have supportive friends and strong families at the ready to help us?* As I plodded through many misadventures trying to find "my people" by going to meetups, social clubs, and support groups and calling hotlines, I grew more discouraged and almost gave up. I did, however, keep a journal, and I began reading alarming and fascinating research on social isolation. Even though the social science research was not the warm and fuzzy reading I preferred at that lonely time, it did validate my experience and explain that I was not the sole cause of my isolation. The research helped me see the bigger picture of how socioeconomic and cultural forces such as social stigma, being financially strapped, or being ill could isolate us.

I still kept looking for self-help books on building or rebuilding one's social life. Most self-help literature tended to put the onus on the individual—to "fix" oneself to attract friends and mates, to make oneself more popular and appealing. According to the self-help industry, the remedy to isolation was self-improvement, making ourselves so likeable, successful, or desirable that we would never be left alone, abandoned, or forgotten.

Indeed, the focus on self-improvement only made me feel lonelier and more ashamed—was I isolated and alone because I just wasn't likeable enough? But wait. What if many of the reasons people were isolated had nothing to do with how likable they were? What if they were suddenly isolated by an unfortunate life event such as a serious illness, losing their home, or losing their spouse? What if everyone's self-absorption with self-improvement was actually keeping them blind to the real barriers in their lives that isolated them?

According to the research (not in the self-help books), isolation could happen to any of us, suddenly, without warning, through no fault of our own. For grappling with the frightening forces of isolation, lonely people like me wanted a self-*acceptance* book, not a self-improvement book!

It was downright unfair that so many good, kind, caring people I had served as a case manager for ten years had been terribly isolated for reasons such as stigma or low status. Too many people on my caseload had been shunned, even by their own families, because they had developmental disabilities, brain injuries, cerebral palsy, or mental illness. Others were isolated due to bereavement after losing spouses, parents, siblings, or other loved ones who had been their caregivers. *Most* of the people on my caseload were isolated because they were poor, sick, old, or homeless. And many family members of those on my caseload were isolated because they were strapped as full-time caregivers.

Suddenly it struck me: with my firsthand experience—both professionally and personally—and in honor of all the lonely people I knew, *I* was the one to write this book. I would call it *400 Friends and No One to Call*, dedicated to those of us who feel isolated even if we are well connected with social media.

400 Friends and No One to Call is a friendly, candid, and practical guide for isolating times when we have no one to talk to. I've woven in my own story of breaking out of isolation by taking my first timid steps toward building a new community of friends in Boston, truly starting from scratch with no one to cheer me on. Because I was writing a book on behalf of vulnerable people like my clients, I was galvanized by a sense of purpose that guided me beyond the grip of my own lonely predicament. Advocating for others who were isolated taught me to advocate for myself, which required my utmost kindness, patience, and fairness. Indeed, in order to befriend my new community, I needed to befriend my own loneliness and fear by being the best self-advocate I could be. As I gradually found my way to new friendships throughout a long, six-year journey, I gained confidence in spelling out how to befriend our wider community, build a social safety net, and foster our sense of belonging.

To better understand how isolation affects us all from a wider perspective, *400 Friends* includes eye-opening social science research. I've been particularly energized by the work of Sherry Turkle, a social science professor at MIT and the author of *Alone Together* (2012) and *Reclaiming Conversation* (2016), who studies how conversation is diminishing in our digital age. I'm also fascinated by how millennials and Generation Z adults are approaching (and avoiding) casual conversation as well as offscreen social activities. A social psychology professor at San Diego State University and author, Dr. Jean Twenge, laments that young adults are "super-connected" in ways that make them overly self-conscious, anxious, and fearful of being judged. It's understandable that the diagnosis of social anxiety is increasing in young adults, which can push them into withdrawal, isolation, and an overreliance on their devices. (Interestingly, I've observed that social anxiety meetups are increasing on Meetup.com with 1,062 groups worldwide—perhaps a heartening sign that shy people are bravely showing up to chat and connect.)

To further inspire us, I've interviewed healthcare providers and clinicians and profiled individuals who've reinvented their entire support systems despite long, lonely periods of isolation. Whether recovering from bereavement, opioid addiction, PTSD, or cancer, they all have heartening news: Social support is out there. Social interventions to fight loneliness are increasing; we're finding one another more easily; and we're growing in numbers. We're weaving together solid safety nets with friends, colleagues, support groups, advocacy groups, meetups, and whole new communities. The trailblazers I've profiled, alongside my own story of breaking out of isolation and building support, offer comforting guidance for isolating times.

By understanding the forces that strap us, scare us, and shame us, we can reach out to others, even when we don't feel strong.

Let's not shy away.

PART ONE

Living IN Isolating Times

CHAPTER ONE

400 Friends and No One to Count On

Isolated in a Digital Age

We can be well-connected, with 400 friends on Facebook, and still have no one to count on. Ironically, despite social media, social isolation is a growing epidemic in the United States. It can grip us at any age, as teenagers shunned on Instagram, as millennials overlooked on dating sites, as families facing an opioid crisis, or seniors living alone with no one checking in on them. The National Science Foundation reported in 2014 that the number of Americans with no close friends has tripled since 1985. One out of four Americans has no one with whom they can confide about their feelings or worries.

Through no fault of our own, we may find ourselves isolated when family members and friends are strapped and stressed, too far away, unavailable, or just not capable. Whom do we call when we have a serious illness, lose our job, a loved one dies, or just need a good, heart-to-heart talk? Having a thoughtful conversation seems too inconvenient and cumbersome for our everyday lives. We hesitate to bother anyone with a friendly phone call or, God forbid, a call for help.

There's hardly time to talk when many of us live in survival mode, paycheck to paycheck, chronic illness to illness, setback to setback. We stay in touch by checking our devices constantly because we expect instant responses from one another. The conveniences of connection set us up to become addicted to connection—or else, we're left out. We feel even more left out when people don't respond with any "Likes" or kind comments. And worse, we compare the responses we receive (or don't) with others who seem much better off. We might be so hell-bent on keeping up with everyone that we grab our mobile device even when a real friend is sitting with us trying to say something meaningful through a dozen interruptions. Distracted and fragmented conversations can be lonely experiences that isolate us, bit by bit.

Social isolation can shatter our confidence. In isolating times, we're not only lonely, but we're ashamed of our loneliness because our society stigmatizes people who are alone without support. We don't want anyone to know how isolated we truly are, so we do whatever it takes to appear happy and well-liked, especially on social media. When we feel this vulnerable, finding new friends in person is not such a simple task. We're hopeless at chitchat so why bother? We're not quite ready to brave our new normal by going solo to a social meetup, taking a cooking class, joining a volleyball team, let alone asking for help in a crisis. Why not just stay home with the comfort of our cat on our lap, Netflix on the screen, and a glass of chardonnay?

Not only does being isolated scare us, but sadly, we might blame ourselves for all the reasons we lack the support of others. Unfortunately, this self-blame for our predicament can isolate us even further. As we try to pinpoint the cause of our isolation with close scrutiny, we find fault with ourselves. Why don't we have more friends? Is something wrong with us?

Aren't we likable? And before we know it, our social confidence is gone, and we are locked in a prison of isolation.

I fell into this vicious cycle of self-blame, relentless scrutiny, and deepening isolation when I survived terribly isolating events back in 2012 and 2013. In the next few pages, I would like to share my story about a powerful revelation that broke me out of my prison of isolation.

My Boston (Not So) Strong Story

As a former rehabilitation counselor and case manager for twenty-two years, I'd guided hundreds of people through isolating times to build support systems in the throes of debilitating illness, grief and loss, unemployment, addiction, domestic abuse, or homelessness. I'd always encouraged the people I served to believe that "it takes a village" to break out of isolation and find the lifelines they needed. I was proud that I could rely on my own resourcefulness and vast social networks and never thought for a second that I was isolated.

But one day, June 1, 2012, at Maine Medical Center, I found myself utterly isolated. I can tell you there is nothing lonelier than waking up in a hospital the day after major surgery and spotting a text message from my friend who canceled and left me stranded. Groggy, sore, and strapped to an IV, I began to realize that no one was showing up to give me a ride home, let alone take care of me once I got home. Though I had carefully made plans with my friend to help after my hysterectomy, I was now left literally to my own devices— my smartphone and the instant connection of social media. Even though I was too weak, wobbly, and dazed to take a taxi home, no one responded to my calls before the nurses discharged me at 3:00 p.m. that day. Alone and deserted, I sat through the night in the hospital lobby watching other people's family members and friends rushing to the elevators to visit their loved ones. Through sheer begging, I finally found a friend of a friend to take me home.

I recovered from my surgery, but my social confidence was shattered. I realized I needed to move to a bigger city like Boston for a better job, affordable health care, and certainly to find more friends. I told everyone I had to "get to Mass to save my ass." But my first year in Boston as a newcomer tested my social confidence and all my beliefs about what it takes to build friendship and community. Indeed, I felt just as invisible and alone there as I had in Maine and assumed this was caused by something wrong with me—my social anxiety. As much as I applied my coping skills with all my knowledge and compassion as a counselor, I still feared my anxiety was the cause of my isolated existence.

And worse, my new job as a case manager at a social services agency did not appear to be a good fit. My supervisor, Lou, was a speedy, multi-tasking millennial, and I was a fifty-eight-year old, conscientious, careful *non-*multitasker. Red-headed and hawkeyed, she bolted through meetings, hurried my questions, and could hardly tolerate training me on Excel spreadsheets. I wondered if she had attention-deficit disorder or if she was doing meth or if she simply hated her job. I pumped myself up to cheerfully ask her to weigh in with my ideas, flyers, letters, budget plans, and reports, but I couldn't get her attention and time.

I shared a desk in a small, cramped office with my coworker, Pat, a case manager around my age who had worked with the agency for sixteen years. Grumpy and territorial, she demanded that I keep my stuff on the left side of our (her) desk, including my bulletin board on the left wall. The first day on my job I politely asked her if I could use a bottom file drawer for my purse, and she remarked, "That's a ridiculous waste of space." I asked where else she thought I might put my purse, and she condescendingly told me to go ask my supervisor because "that's not my decision."

But as a highly sensitive introvert who needed a quiet spot to focus, I just couldn't concentrate well enough to get work done. Lou was beginning to show her displeasure with how "meticulous" I was and that I needed to "just get it done." I even detected a sarcastic, passive-aggressive form of hostility coming toward me from both Lou and Pat. Had they preferred someone else for the job, but got stuck with me for some reason beyond their control? Or was I just too fastidious for them?

My long, chronic illness of colitis flared up with the work stress, keeping me up most nights. I lost my energy and mental clarity, and soon my social anxiety kicked in. Pat and Lou could plainly see that I was a nervous wreck and that I must be sick. I began to avoid them and keep a low profile, just so I could get my work done, but I wasn't keeping up. By my fourth week on the job, I feared they might ask me to quit.

But one afternoon, on April 15, 2013, everything stopped when we heard about the Boston Marathon Bombing through text messages. We rushed home in our own separate ways and stayed home through the days when the city was locked down, glued to our TV sets.

Once the worst of the disaster was over and the second Tsarnaev brother had been arrested, the all-clear was given and somehow all Bostonians could go back to work. With a Dunkin Donuts coffee in hand, like thousands of people in Massachusetts returning to work that morning, I was supposedly ready to get back to normal at my desk. But I dreaded this whole day and strategically decided to just numb myself and hide in a small conference room, doing a little paperwork and calling to reschedule meetings. I could see Pat in the distance, walking slowly down the hall, stirring her instant oatmeal in a bowl. I almost wanted to approach her and check in, but I figured it was safer to stay in the background.

Two hours slowly drifted by, and I got up to stretch. Lou was not coming in that day, according to her text. Thank God, I breathed. I wondered why I hadn't heard a sound from Pat's office. She usually spoke loudly on her phone calls. With a sudden surge of curiosity, I strolled over to peek into Pat's office to see if she was still there. She was. She didn't see me. I paused to mentally rehearse what I'd say to her. At least I'd ask how she was doing. And just let her know I would be in the conference room catching up on paperwork.

I stepped to the doorway, and noticed Pat had her head in her hands and was slumped over her desk. Her hands were in fists, and she was deep in thought. I hesitated again—perhaps I shouldn't disturb her. But she looked troubled, and it didn't seem right to just walk away.

I called out, "Hello, Pat. How's it going?"

She glanced at me and then looked down and sighed. "I'm doing pretty crappy to tell the truth."

"Is it because of the bombing?" I ventured to ask.

"I can't get a damn bit of work done today. I shouldn't have come in. I'm still not over it. I can't get my mind off of it."

"It's horrible." I meekly responded.

"I just can't get my mind off my son. He was *there*. He saw his friend get blown up. He saw his friend almost lose his arm. He saw his friend in agony and he felt helpless. He still feels helpless."

"Awful. Just . . . terrible for your son to witness. I'm so sorry to hear this."

"My son is totally freaked out. He told me he wants to go see his friend at the hospital but he's afraid he has nothing to say or he might say something stupid. He feels so paralyzed and guilty."

"Thank God at least he talks to you, Pat. At least he's not holding all those feelings inside by himself."

"Please don't tell me to take him to a therapist. I hate it when people say to go to a damn therapist when they're too scared to 'go there' with you. You know what I mean?"

"God, no, Pat, I won't tell you to go to a therapist. It sucks, I agree, when people cop out like that."

"Yeah, but now I don't know what to tell him. I have no clue and I'm his mother. I don't know what to say. There are no words to express how horrible this is for him—or for his friend or his friend's family. There are no words. So, what in hell do you do?"

"Did you say he hasn't gone to the hospital to visit him yet?"

"No. I know that's not good. He should have gone right away. But he has just shut down."

Our conversation stopped for a minute. I immediately thought of my time lying alone in the hospital in Maine, isolated, stranded, afraid. There was nothing worse than no one showing up.

Suddenly, surprising myself, I blurted out loud my truth: "There is nothing lonelier than lying in a hospital bed when no one shows up."

Pat was intrigued. "You're right. I agree. It must be awful to lie in that hospital thinking your friends don't give a rat's ass about you."

I didn't tell Pat my story, but she clearly understood my message. "That's right, Pat. To be totally blunt, you need to tell your son to get to that hospital ASAP. He doesn't have to say anything. He just needs to show up. That's all. His friend will be glad he cared enough to visit, even if he doesn't know what to say. Maybe there just isn't anything to say."

Pat nodded slowly. "My son has got to go see him. I'm going to tell him what you said. He needs to understand how lonely it is when people don't show up. I will tell him it's okay if he doesn't have anything to say. Just show up and you've already done the most important thing."

"I'm glad. I bet he'll go, Pat. He can't just leave his friend there all day."

"And I can always give him a ride or just go *with* him. At least he would be less likely to chicken out!" Pat chuckled.

I laughed. "You have your work cut out for you. Good luck!"

She softly and shyly thanked me. "Thanks . . . I appreciate your help today, Val. I'm going to talk to my son this evening."

Pat and I decided we weren't going to get any more work done that day. She left before I did. I sat at her desk and marveled at how the ice had been broken between us. Pat wasn't just that grouchy coworker who sarcastically complained about me, and I wasn't the loser who couldn't manage her job. She was in pain about her son, and I couldn't walk away. In a sad but tender way, the aftermath of the marathon bombing had released us from the constraints of the normal, strained, competitive roles we played at work. Today, we were two women in shock from what our city had suffered. Our office today was a safe place for us to share our vulnerability. I remembered 9/11 and how we as Americans, for a few days or weeks, even at our jobs, shared our humility, humanity, and compassion. Unfortunately, this sanctuary of caring was only a respite for a brief period and faded too soon. I figured in another week or two Pat and I might drift back into our tensions and defenses. But at least we had today as a foundation of trust.

One week later, to my joyous surprise, Pat approached me with good news. Her son had mustered up the wherewithal to go see his friend at Mass General Hospital. Not only had he visited his friend, but his friend had introduced him to other wounded victims of the bombing in neighboring rooms. Pat proudly reported that he had "bonded" with these guys and was now "partying" with them. He had made new friends by showing up, even without the right words to say.

Pat beamed. "He's matured five years in one week. He said something amazing yesterday: 'Boston Strong doesn't mean you have to be strong to show up for your friends. It just means you have to show up, period.'"

Her son had it right. Brilliant. It struck me that my Boston Strong experience was not about being strong, but about showing up. You don't have to be strong to reach out and care. It doesn't require strength, courage, smarts, or confidence. What it does take is knowing how bad it feels to be left alone and hurting. All we want is someone to show up. I had learned this lesson on that terrible day when stranded at Maine Medical Center, and thankfully, the painful truth of my experience had enabled me to help Pat, her son, and his friends.

How fortunate we are that our pain can be transformed into wisdom that helps another person. We can break through isolation by showing up, even if we're not strong or we lack confidence. It never hurts to wear the big pants—to give support even when we need support. And we just might be surprised what happens next.

Myths about Social Isolation That Hurt Us

My experience with Pat was one of a few life-changing breakthroughs that healed me after years of isolation. For each of my hard-won revelations that broke me out of the prison of isolation, an underlying myth had to be busted. These myths had misled me and kept me isolated, echoing the harsh social stigma in our culture about being alone.

It's so tragic that we often blame and judge ourselves with social stigma in isolating times. Indeed, we often turn against ourselves at the very moment we need to turn to others. The myths and beliefs echoing this stigma can shatter our social confidence, destroying the courage, hope, and wherewithal we need for venturing into new relationships.

The myths on the following pages can isolate us and commonly stem from social stigma:

MYTHS	REVELATIONS
You're alone because you've failed at relationships.	We all can feel this way, though we appear "normal."
You're alone because there is something wrong with you.	Many of us are isolated through no fault of our own.
There is a reason you ended up alone.	Both external and internal forces cause isolation.
You must hide your loneliness so you don't bring others down.	It is essential to find a safe person for sharing our vulnerability. We might need to call a helpline, find a support group, therapist, or chaplain.
Don't ever tell your friends, family or anyone how lonely you are.	
Loneliness is embarrassing and shameful.	We can befriend our loneliness with self-compassion.

Why am I isolated?

MYTHS	REVELATIONS
You alone are to blame for your isolation.	Blame isolates us further.
Your isolation is caused only by your character flaws.	See the big picture, beyond your own flaws.
If you had planned better, made better choices, picked better friends, found a better partner, saved your money, done things differently, you wouldn't be so isolated.	Forces greater than ourselves can isolate us. Living in survival mode can isolate us (severe illness, financial loss, bereavement, natural disasters, and other devastating events).

I need to get out more, but . . .

MYTHS	REVELATIONS
Getting out and exploring is no fun if you're alone.	Follow your curiosity, even if you're alone.
You look like a loser if you go out to places by yourself.	Enjoy and explore your community. Take photos, take a tour, start a blog, walk dogs, people-watch, smell roses. You might be surprised who you meet.

How do I (dare I) ask for help?

MYTHS	REVELATIONS
People will think you're needy if you ask for help.	Become an advocate for yourself and others.
People will judge you if you ask for help.	Ask for help from people who have been through similar hardships themselves. Reach out to a helpline or support group. You're in charge even if you're the one asking for help. Be specific and clear with requests.
You shouldn't burden people. You might scare them away.	Keep it practical and tangible. Avoid asking too much of any one person. Break it down into steps.

What if I can't count on my friends or family?

MYTHS	REVELATIONS
You should only count on your family and closest friends.	It takes a village to build a solid support system.
You should have family and friends to count on, or else something is wrong with you or wrong with them.	No matter how strong (or not) our families or friends are, we all go through isolating times.
People who have no one except support groups are losers.	
People who have no one except therapists are losers.	
Only a few people can be real friends.	Support is all around us when we befriend our communities, from coworkers to cousins to neighbors to hairstylists to Uber drivers to volleyball teams to our cats and dogs.

Showing Up and Reaching Out

MYTHS	REVELATIONS
When you feel uncertain, awkward, or afraid, you shouldn't reach out to others—you might say or do the wrong thing.	Most people appreciate our interest and caring.

You're probably intruding if you show up or reach out.	Our interest and caring can carry us beyond our fears.
You should avoid reaching out to people who are different than you are because you might offend or hurt them.	We don't have to feel strong to show that we care.
	We get support when we give support—it can work both ways.

Social Media and Social Isolation

MYTHS	REVELATIONS
When you're well-connected on social media you always have someone to call in a crisis.	We can have 400 friends on Facebook and no one to call.
Social media means you have a solid support system.	Even though it helps to connect and organize people through social media, we need face-to-face connections and hands-on support. We need to "be there" in person.
The more "likes" you have on Facebook, the more likeable you really are. And if you don't get any "likes," then no one cares about you.	I am loved by someone; I have been loved by someone.

Special Observations for People over Fifty

MYTHS	REVELATIONS
At your age, you should have lots of friends to rely on.	As it turns out, many of us might need to start all over again to build social support—at sixty, seventy, or eighty.
You've spent five or six decades building relationships so you should be able to enjoy wonderful relationships by now.	It takes lots of work building (and keeping) relationships at any age. Darn—it might not get easier with age. But maybe we become more patient and forgiving with each other.
Older adults don't have the energy and stamina for new relationships.	When we are truly interested in others, we find a way to connect. Love gives us a boost, and we might be surprised how our energy rebounds.

Special Observations for Introverts and Highly Sensitive People

MYTHS	REVELATIONS
Introverts are isolated, and they like it that way.	Introverts need deep, meaningful connections. Being isolated feels different than quiet time alone.
You should always avoid groups.	Some groups (meetups) are designed for introverts by introverts, highly sensitive people, empaths, and other old souls. We need to meet each other to survive this noisy, extroverted, busy world.
You're always misunderstood so you should keep your mouth shut.	There are many ways to communicate even if we don't talk a lot. Plus, people love a good listener.

Special Observations for Single and/or Childless People

MYTHS	REVELATIONS
People with spouses, partners, or families aren't isolated and lonely.	Even in a so-called "happy marriage," people can feel alone and unsupported sometimes. They need their single friends to help them through these times.
Most couples don't care enough to understand single people.	Even our fellow single friends might not understand us at times. Single or not, most people care and try.
People who have kids are judgmental toward people who don't have kids.	Some of our friends with children are breaking through the old stigma by getting to know us as a unique person (beyond roles). Let them know how dear their friendship is to you and keep reaching out.

As we reflect on the myths that keep us isolated, we can understand why we have tried to avoid being judged, shamed, or shunned by holding ourselves back from reaching out to others. It may seem simple and obvious that the answer to breaking out of isolation is to "get out more," such as volunteering at the YMCA, joining a sports team, or taking a class, but it's not so simple when these myths and beliefs play havoc with our social confidence. The more we are aware of how these deeply ingrained patterns hold us back from reaching out and building the support we need, the more patient, compassionate, and accepting we can become with ourselves and one another.

Complicating the ways these myths affect us, unfortunately, social media can intensify, exploit, and even weaponize social stigma. Every day we observe mean-spirited remarks and try to numb ourselves, accepting that this stigmatizing, shaming, and disrespect comes with the territory of our digital age. But the sting of this inhumanity sneaks up on us in our most vulnerable times. Any one of us can instantly be deleted or unfriended from someone's life with no warning, no explanation, let alone a single, caring word. It's tragic yet understandable how a fragile teen, a struggling addict, or a lonely baby boomer could turn this cold, dehumanizing act of unfriending against themselves and become more withdrawn, even suicidal. But even if we aren't so fragile, in our loneliest, most isolated times it still hurts when we don't get a single "Like," someone deletes us, or someone harshly comments on our post.

I can personally attest to being sensitive to the inhumanity of social media after a hard, exhausting day at work as a counselor trying to soothe angry or anxious families. When I got home and checked in with Facebook last week, I didn't have a clue why someone I truly liked and admired had just unfriended me. I instantly fell into the same self-doubt that a thirteen-year old feels when her classmates have rejected her. And yet, in just minutes, those dark feelings disappeared when I remembered I'd been invited by a dear friend to dinner the next day. I swelled with joy and gratitude that this hard-won relationship had taken a lot of love, work, patience, and forgiveness. Thank goodness, I smiled, for my true friends! This is the real stuff, the good stuff—not that other stuff online. It's so brutally obvious how social media can make us feel inadequate and how our loving, face-to-face relationships are essential to our sense of belonging in this world.

Thanks to the revelations of my long journey out of isolation and what I've witnessed from twenty-four years of counseling with severely isolated people, I feel heartened and ready to share what I've learned about building stronger support networks. We need our wider communities of support now more than ever as a buffer to social media, stigma, the lack of face-to-face conversation, and the harshness of our world. It's a hard world to be soft in.

The Stigma of Loneliness: A Self-Assessment

Social stigma and stereotypes about isolated and lonely people can affect our attitudes toward *ourselves* about being lonely or isolated. It's interesting and revealing to review how our own beliefs might be influenced by our culture. Below is a list of ten questions that can allow you to examine your true feelings and biases about loneliness and isolation. There are no right or wrong answers—we're exploring our gut feelings about an awkward topic that we hardly discuss in our culture.

Which answer best reflects your *first* thought or reaction?

1. **You see a well-dressed middle-aged woman eating dinner alone at a nice restaurant.**

   a. I feel sorry for her.

   b. It makes me uncomfortable. I avoid eye contact with her.

   c. It's fine, but I'd rather not be in her shoes.

   d. I wish I had the guts to go out by myself like that.

   e. It's good to pamper ourselves and go out for a wonderful meal.

2. **A pleasant sixty-five-year-old friend of a friend you've known for a few months emails you to ask if he could have a ride home from his colonoscopy in two weeks. He explains that he recently moved to your city and his only friend is working that day and not available. You have no firm plans that day.**

   a. No way. It's just not appropriate to ask anyone other than family members or close friends for a favor.

   b. It's a red flag of warning that he has hardly any friends—safer not to respond and delete his email.

   c. His friend should have contacted me first to give me a heads up. This seems dicey. Don't think so.

   d. Maybe I can help, but this feels awkward. I will contact my friend who knows him well and ask more about him before I make a decision.

   e. He's in a tough situation. He'll be too groggy to use Uber to get home. Sure, I'll give him a lift.

3. **Lonely people I've known have appeared needy sometimes. I've deliberately avoided conversations with them or else I might get sucked in to more than I can handle.**

   a. Very true—I avoid them. They can be draining "energy vampires."

   b. I feel uncomfortable, but I try to be compassionate. I avoid them by finding a nice excuse to get away.

   c. I feel sorry for them, but I chat a bit just to be polite.

   d. I care because I know what it feels like to be alone. Still, I'm careful to keep the conversation light and noncommittal.

   e. I usually enjoy chatting with anybody, lonely or not. I can gently let them know when I need to leave.

4. I'm a little suspicious about becoming friends with someone who talks more about their pets than their human relationships.

a. Very true.

b. Somewhat true.

c. Occasionally.

d. It doesn't bother me. I guess they're just introverted.

e. Maybe I could ask a little more about them. They might be shy and only feel safe talking about their pets.

5. I believe most people are isolated because they have somehow alienated others by certain behaviors or personalities.

a. I strongly agree.

b. I generally agree.

c. I believe that about half the people out there are honest and good people who are isolated for reasons beyond their control. But the other half—probably there's a reason they've ended up alone.

d. I mostly disagree.

e. I strongly disagree.

6. People should count on their families, first and foremost.

a. Right. If we can't rely on our families, then something is terribly wrong with this world.

b. I mostly agree. I tend to be suspicious of people who say they don't have a family or they're not close to their family.

c. I find it sad when people don't have family members to turn to.

d. I just don't believe in saying "should." I think it's best not to have expectations of our family members to be there for us—or expect anyone to be there for us.

e. It's wonderful to have supportive families, but more and more of us need our wider communities *in addition* to our families. It takes a village.

7. Most people who are isolated *chose* to be isolated.

   a. I mostly agree.

   b. I somewhat agree.

   c. I would say that about half the people I know who are isolated have deliberately chosen to withdraw.

   d. Most of us don't choose to be isolated. Perhaps they are suffering from social anxiety or depression.

   e. Both internal and external forces isolate us—and these forces play off each other.

8. Support groups are usually full of lonely, neurotic people complaining and venting.

   a. I feel exactly the same way about most support groups.

   b. I know support groups are helpful, but I'd rather not share my feelings with a group of vulnerable people.

   c. I'm hesitant, but I'll try one. I've had mixed experiences in the past with support groups. Some people at groups can be real downers.

   d. I'm interested and willing to go to one, but I won't go more than once if it doesn't meet my needs.

   e. I'm happy to find a group. I've had mostly positive experiences in the past with support groups.

9. At work one day, a young, friendly coworker in his early twenties approaches you to ask if he can borrow $5.00 to help him with

the gas money to drive home. He is quite humble and shy about asking you to help and promises to pay you back when he gets his paycheck. He says he is afraid to ask his supervisor. He has been at this job for two weeks. You actually do have some cash in your wallet.

a. I would prefer not to lend him the money because I don't know what I might be getting into. I tell him that I'm sorry, but I don't have the money. I suggest he goes to speak to the payroll staff about a possible advance.

b. I'm wary. I might help him, but first I ask if he has any family members or friends he might call.

c. I'm not comfortable with helping him, but I still give him the $5.00 he needs.

d. It's okay with me, but just this one time. I give him the $5.00.

e. I give him the $5.00. I reassure him that I know how it feels to start a new job and get back on your own feet.

10. **You see a middle-aged woman of a different race than yours at a party sitting alone in a wheel chair. She appears awkward and self-conscious, but shyly offers a smile when you make eye contact with her. You gently approach her, kindly ask her name, and begin a brief conversation.**

a. I admit I don't tend to walk up to people who are by themselves at social occasions.

b. I feel sorry for her. I smile and say, "Hi," but not much more because I feel awkward as well.

c. I might go sit with that person and briefly chat, just to be polite and do the right thing.

d. I would like to sit and chat with her because I'm curious to find out if she is new to the area.

e. I think people who come solo to parties are interesting. I would enjoy getting to know her.

Of the previous ten questions, if you answered Ds or Es for six or more questions, you probably have a more open and accepting attitude toward being lonely or isolated. If you tended to answer with As or Bs for six or more questions, you could be a bit judgmental with yourself when you feel lonely or isolated. If you answered mostly Cs, you are in the middle.

Did you notice your biases about people who seem lonely or isolated? Did reflecting on these scenarios touch on any feelings of shame, fear, or anxiety about your own loneliness and isolation? It's important to remember that we are all affected by social stigma—and we often turn it against ourselves. This is why it's not so easy to "get out there" when we want to rebuild our support networks, search for new friends, or meet possible romantic partners. Before we set out to build new relationships, it helps to build a compassionate relationship with our own loneliness. Indeed, befriending our loneliness is a big step to accepting ourselves amid the stigma and judgment around us.

For the next set of ten questions, we examine our feelings about social media and our digital culture. Most of us appreciate how social media can help us locate ways to get connected when we are building new support networks, but we also know the downside: It might make us feel bad about ourselves—and even worse when we're lonely and isolated.

Which answer best reflects your *first* thought or impression?

1. I admit that getting "Likes" on social media makes me feel better. And if I don't get any responses at all, I worry.

a. Yes, that's often true for me.

b. It depends on my mood. On some days, people's responses affect me.

c. I could take it or leave it. It's nice to get the "Likes," but it doesn't get me down if I don't get them.

d. I could care less. I hardly notice the responses.

e. I post interesting or helpful articles that I want to share, regardless of how people react.

2. **Our cell phones are making people flaky these days. You name it—friends, coworkers, family members—everyone breaks commitments too often. It seems more commonplace now for people to over-promise and then back out at the last minute.**

a. There have always been flaky people, in any generation.

b. I don't think it's flakiness. People are downright rude these days.

c. Our phones are making us flakier.

d. Flakiness is a whole epidemic now. Everyone is overwhelmed.

e. All of the above.

3. **Whenever I've been unfriended or deleted, it has hurt my feelings.**

a. That's always true for me, it hurts no matter how close or not I am to that person.

b. Sometimes—it depends on how well I know the person.

c. It doesn't hurt too much, but it makes me ruminate about what I might have said or done.

d. I don't take it personally. It's just part of living with social media. (But it does make me curious about why this person did this.)

e. It doesn't affect me at all. I don't give it much thought.

4. **I've waited a month to have lunch with a dear friend, and I'm jazzed about our visit. We finally sit down at our favorite restaurant and begin to catch up with our news. In ten minutes, she excuses herself to check on a text message. I'm frustrated. Can't we at least have an hour of face time without interruptions?**

   a. I would feel the same way.

   b. I'm annoyed, but I take a deep breath and try to accept that this is life in digital times. "It is what it is."

   c. I don't like it, but I've gotten used to my friends and loved ones doing this all the time.

   d. I'm okay with it. I take a moment to look around and people-watch.

   e. I check my messages.

5. **I'm often envious of what my friends post on Facebook. For example, only *one* person bothered to send me a birthday wish. But all the time I see *dozens* of people responding to my friend's birthdays!**

   a. I would feel the same way. Maybe people don't care that much about me.

   b. I would wonder why I didn't receive more birthday wishes.

   c. I try not to let it get to me. I'll send a nice message to the one person who did wish me a happy birthday.

   d. Oh, just screw it. It's only Facebook.

   e. I have plenty of real friends who hardly use Facebook.

6. **I sometimes feel left out or inadequate when I compare myself to others on social media—better family life, taking nice vacations, great jobs, having fun socializing . . .**

   a. I often feel inadequate.

b. It sometimes affects me.

c. I know that people are only *selectively* sharing their stuff, but still, it gets to me a little.

d. I don't feel left out. I always like to see how my friends are doing. I cheer them on with "Likes."

e. I really enjoy all the positive energy from their happy photos.

7. **I've become more assertive about insisting we take a break from our devices, especially at dinner time. If I'm bothering to cook a nice dinner for everyone, then we'd *better* enjoy being at the table together without interruptions!**

a. I've tried, but I'm lucky to get even twenty minutes of face time any given day.

b. I've tried, and I'm lucky to get maybe forty minutes of face time during the day.

c. I've tried and at least on some days, we can go a whole hour with face time.

d. I don't have to try too hard. We've found good times to talk.

e. My friends and family are totally on board with making face time sacred. It's our sanctuary from the world.

8. **In our digital age, I believe it's much more difficult to have deep or meaningful conversations with anyone. I miss having long, heart-to-heart talks about the important things in life. Sometimes I feel lonely not being able to share my deepest thoughts and feelings with others.**

a. Very true for me. I feel sad and discouraged that the world seems so superficial and fast-paced.

b. Somewhat true for me. I try to find other outlets for my feelings if I can't talk to anyone about them.

c. This gets to me sometimes, but I'm an optimist and believe humans are evolving in ways we can't always understand.

d. I think the world has always seemed superficial to deep thinkers and "old souls." We can always find our kindred spirits.

e. We can live creatively and be open and grateful. Things have a way of working out in the end.

9. I don't think I fit in our digital age. I feel like an outsider. I'm more isolated than ever.

a. True. It's a lonely world out there. I wish I had real friends.

b. Sometimes I feel this way. But I have at least a couple of friends who understand.

c. We must adapt to the digital world or we will be left in the dust.

d. I believe in compromise and balance. We can spend some time online and other time offline.

e. I believe we can connect even more deeply and honestly online. We can blog and share all kinds of insights, feelings, dreams, observations. Let's get creative online!

10. Reflect for a moment: Over the past ten years, do you believe social media has made you feel more lonely or less lonely?

a. Definitely more lonely.

b. Somewhat more lonely than I'd like.

c. I feel about the same, not more lonely or less lonely.

d. Somewhat less lonely.

e. Definitely less lonely.

If six or more of your answers were Ds or Es, you are likely to be less sensitive to the effects of our digital age and social media. If you answered with six or more As and Bs, social media and our digital culture might be affecting how isolated and lonely you feel. If you have many Cs or were evenly split with your answers, you have mixed feelings and live with ambivalence.

It's helpful to pay attention to our values, beliefs, and feelings about social media so we don't allow it to dictate whether or not we "fit in." Hopefully, we're not allowing social media to define our sense of belonging in the world. I found it liberating one day to reclaim my sense of belonging by decorating beautiful handmade cards and writing gratitude messages to each of my loved ones, friends, and closest colleagues. I told each of them how they had helped me hold onto a true sense of belonging despite how social media had lured me into doubting my reputation, status, and self-worth.

It's also helped me to read social science research about the effects of stigma and social media on social isolation. I've discovered vital and eye-opening research to enhance my understanding of the common ways we're all influenced in our culture. Learning what social science is telling us can be validating for any of us healing from a bitterly lonely time. In the next chapter I will briefly explore some socioeconomic and cultural forces that isolate us. Understanding the bigger picture can give us a more compassionate and informed perspective on why so many of us feel isolated and what we can do to build a social safety net of support for ourselves and one another.

CHAPTER TWO

The Forces
That Isolate Us

The Big Picture of Isolation: Socioeconomic and Cultural Forces

Just hearing the word "isolation" conjures up images of lonely, abandoned spaces, confinement, separation, alienation. It feels dark and cold. According to the *Oxford English Dictionary*, to "isolate" means "to cause to be alone or apart." Social isolation is an absence of contact between an individual and society.

Isolation is different than loneliness, a perceived state of isolation (we *feel* isolated when we are lonely, even though we may be surrounded by others). Socially isolated people suffer serious barriers to social contact (such as the lack of transportation or the inability to access social events due to a disability) and have endured a severe lack of social support. In contrast, loneliness is a common reaction to a personal sense of isolation—of not belonging, not feeling included, not being accepted, understood, or loved. Socially isolated people are usually lonely, but not always. Social science research examines both "perceived" isolation (a sense of isolation or loneliness) and "actual" isolation (an objective lack of human contact) to understand how isolation and loneliness interact.

In common terms, when we use the word "isolate" we mean *cause* to isolate or to isolate *ourselves*. Furthermore, when we say, "You're isolating yourself," we are placing the blame on the individual. We are implying that this person too often *chooses* to withdraw from people, which most of us believe is an unhealthy habit. Our societal verdict: Something is wrong with those who isolate themselves on a regular basis.

Extroverts often view introverts as being too isolated. Introverts usually prefer spending time alone and quiet time for reflection. (As a highly sensitive and introverted writer, I understand this well: I crave long, peaceful retreats for deep concentration and reflection.) But there is a great difference between our need for quiet time alone and being truly isolated. Introverts as well as extroverts can choose to get out and connect when we feel up to it, and we often have at least one friend with whom we can confide. Introverts are typically not isolated, but they are more private with their connections.

Unfortunately, the self-help industry over the past two decades has turned the popular use of the term "isolating" into a negative label, describing a pattern of withdrawing from others. Supposedly we fall into escapist routines and retreat from the world, aided by the devices of our digital age to keep ourselves free from the burdens of others. Many of us have been accused of isolating when our friends noticed we weren't getting out as much. Alarmed by their observations, we may have reacted with self-judgment, self-doubt, or shame. And before we know it, we've blamed ourselves for all the reasons we're isolated.

But social isolation is not always a choice. And our singular focus on self-blame for our isolation may be blinding us from the greater realities of our lives that truly isolate us—and can isolate *any* of us. If we take a quick look at an AARP study of isolation in people over age fifty, for example, it's clear that forces stronger than ourselves can cause isolation.

Here are eight of the top reasons people over fifty are isolated (in no particular order), according to AARP's Connect2Affect studies (2012–2017). Some of these factors certainly apply to those younger than fifty:

1. Living alone (nearly 30 percent of adults over sixty are living alone).
2. Poor health and well-being (mobility or sensory impairment).
3. Major life transitions and losses such as bereavement, separation, or divorce.
4. Socioeconomic status, lack of access to opportunities, inequality (loss of income, limited resources).
5. Location (rural, unsafe, or inaccessible neighborhoods).
6. Being a caregiver for someone with a disability or serious illness.
7. Transportation challenges.
8. Societal barriers, stigma, bias toward certain social groups (ageism, sexism, racism, ableism/people with disabilities, others).

Millennials may be even more isolated. According to a recent Cigna study, the loneliest age group is composed of those eighteen to twenty years old, Generation Z. The second loneliest is the twenty-three to thirty-seven age group.

The 2018 Cigna survey of more than 20,000 US adults ages eighteen years and older revealed these eye-opening findings:

- **Generation Z (adults ages eighteen to twenty-two)** is the loneliest generation and claims to be in worse health than older generations.
- **Nearly half** of Americans report sometimes or always feeling alone (46 percent) or left out (47 percent).
- **One in four** Americans (27 percent) rarely or never feel as though there are people who really understand them.

- **Two in five** Americans sometimes or always feel that their relationships are not meaningful (43 percent) and that they are isolated from others (43 percent).
- **One in five** people report they rarely or never feel close to people (20 percent) or feel like there are people they can talk to (18 percent).
- **Americans who live with others are less likely to be lonely** (average loneliness score of 43.5) compared to those who live alone (46.4). However, this does not apply to single parents/guardians (average loneliness score of 48.2). Even though they live with children, they are more likely to be lonely.

In my case, in 2012, before I moved to Boston from Portland, Maine, I was living alone, broke, single, in the throes of having my job cut to half time, struggling with a serious disease called colitis, and my very old car was breaking down. I'd hardly a cent to get down the road, let alone get out to "socialize." I certainly couldn't go out for sushi with my better-off friends, and even McDonalds was too costly. And with the flare-ups of chronic colitis I was weak and fatigued, barely able to keep up at my job, even though I didn't "look sick." I relied more on social media to stay connected because getting out was just not possible for me. Was I really isolating or was I just downright strapped in survival mode? Was it fair that some friends claimed I was isolating, or did they just not understand my plight having never been so broke themselves nor worn down by a chronic illness?

People in dire survival mode are often judged by friends, colleagues, or family members for isolating. Unfortunately, instead of honestly explaining to our loved ones the barriers to getting out more (which we might fear appears as whining), we often give in to their judgment. We can internalize their judgment and harshly blame our introversion, our anxiety, our lack of planning, our lack of savings, or our "poor choices" in jobs, neighborhoods, partners, or friends.

Sadly, in 2012, I blamed myself for my isolation, and concluded that I was doing a poor job of reaching out to others. My friends must be right—I wasn't trying hard enough. According to them, admitting forces beyond my control was a cop-out, giving in to defeat. It was easier to simply blame my isolation on character flaws rather than to honestly and compassionately accept that my life had drastically changed due to a debilitating illness and to losing half my income. Unfortunately, turning to self-help books further reinforced the belief that healing isolation is simply a matter of fixing oneself, improving oneself, making oneself more likeable, which made me feel *worse*. All the self-help books, spiritual books, and wellness books I read, and all the advice I'd ever been given, told me there was no excuse for being isolated—it was *all* about attitude—until June 1, 2012, when I woke up at Maine Medical Center after my surgery.

Being stranded in the hospital after my hysterectomy was my wake-up call that I was truly isolated, and that isolation could happen to any of us, no matter how well-organized, well-connected, or well-loved we might be. My friend Becky had agreed to pick me up from the hospital and stay with me overnight. I was counting on her, my most reliable and kindest friend, to show up. In the eleven years I'd known her, we'd never let each other down. I'd taken care of her cats, her garden, her mail, and her phone messages when she was away, and she had taken me to occasional medical procedures.

But on the one day I needed her most, as I reached across my hospital bed while the nurse changed my IV, I spotted on my mobile a strange, short text: "So sorry—family emergency—cannot come today."

Holding my phone in front of my face like a mirror, I stared in shock at her text message, reading the same few words over and over. Becky was not showing up. No one was showing up. Instead of anger, I felt petrified, helpless, and ashamed that I had no one to count on.

Hunting for people to take care of me shattered my dignity, but I still had faith that Becky was my friend. I was willing to forgive her for not showing up at the hospital because I figured her ailing father with dementia was in a crisis and she had rushed down to Rhode Island.

But Becky didn't return any of my phone calls or emails for days after I got home. She completely disappeared. I was worried about her and desperate to know what the hell had happened. What was her emergency all about? The human resources staff at her job told me she was working that day with their agency. So, she was back at work after whatever had happened but ignoring my messages. Why was she avoiding me? What was going on? Had I done something wrong?

As weeks turned into months with no response from Becky, I grew bitter and cynical. Even my other friends seemed distant. My friends had always been my true family as I'd never been able to count on my own family of origin. But now, after five decades of building friendships, I had no one to turn to.

Finally, many months later, I learned from one of Becky's friends why she hadn't shown up on the day I was in the hospital. Her daughter had been in a car accident and was in the ER at a hospital 200 miles away. Becky had dashed off early that morning because no one else could take over the crisis.

After I heard the news, I phoned Becky again and left a compassionate voice mail as a message of concern, but she never responded. Finally, I realized I would have to let her go. But it broke my heart that I could never tell her in person that I was relieved her daughter had survived or that I forgave her for not showing up at the hospital on that terrible day.

I hadn't realized at this time that at the root of Becky's withdrawal from me was a dark secret that isolated her from all of her friends. Two of her adult stepchildren were addicted to opioids, causing perpetual crisis and chaos in all aspects of Becky's life. It struck me that Becky was trapped by a brutal disease that tears families and friendships apart—a relationship killer. It can ruin trust, our promises and best intentions, commitments, dreams, and the love we long to share. And in my case, opioid addiction threatened to destroy my friendship with Becky. Indeed, she was more isolated than I was, even though she had a large family, as she was locked in relentless, exhausting turmoil. For all the twelve-step programs Becky attended, for all the counseling and self-help books, and for all the antidepressant medications she tried, nothing could free her from her prison of self-blame.

I turned to reading social science research on addiction, which led to the topic of social isolation. I wasn't shocked to learn that social isolation was a serious, fast-increasing epidemic observed by medical providers throughout the US. And the opioid crisis certainly is part and parcel of our isolating times. Study after study reveals that families of addicts can be just as isolated as addicts themselves, due to social stigma, shame, and other stressors such as financial or medical demands.

The research I studied and understanding Becky's crisis, softened my expectations of how people should "be there" for each other. Indeed, she had left me stranded in the hospital and left me stranded as a friend because *she* was stranded by the opioid crisis that was decimating her family. What goes around comes around, this epidemic of being stranded and disappearing. Any one of us can be stranded. And any one of us could be the one who leaves someone stranded for reasons beyond our control.

My ordeal with Becky revealed to me how external forces in our lives can isolate us, or at least contribute to isolation, and blaming ourselves or each other never works. I can see clearly how social isolation is complicated by both situational (external) forces as well as psychological (internal) forces.

And the interplay between these forces causes a painful, downward spiral of isolation.

Here are some common causes of social isolation:

SITUATIONAL BARRIERS	INTERNAL BARRIERS
Illness, chronic pain, or disability	Anxiety
Financial loss, unemployment	Avoidance of being hurt again
Caregiving demands	Depression, hopelessness
Working too many hours/ financial hardship	Bitterness, alienation, disgust with humanity
Loss of a home, frequent moves, living in unsafe areas	Extreme introversion, no close contacts
Transportation barriers	Impatience, impulsivity
Loss, bereavement, or separation from a loved one	Shame
Relocation, being new to a community	Blame and self-blame
Empty nest after a child leaves home	High sensitivity
Retirement, lacking connection with coworkers	Lack of interest in others, self-absorption
Aging, losing many loved ones and being left alone	Cognitive and intellectual deficits
Suddenly becoming famous or successful (outshining peers)	Lack of empathy
Language and cultural barriers	Resistance to change, inflexibility, close-mindedness
Being exceptionally gifted or talented (threatening to others)	Lack of curiosity for the world outside of ourselves
Isolation or estrangement from an abusive partner or family member	Attachment to relationships that have ended
Being a family member, parent, or child of an addict	Addiction, chemical dependency

This is not a conclusive list, of course, but we can review common reasons why we find ourselves isolated or lonely. Given the situational and internal reasons for our isolation, it's wise to put in perspective the fact that we are living in an age of increasing isolation, in the US as well as the world. We may have observed how isolated our loved ones, friends, or colleagues have become, and how difficult it is to break through the forces isolating one another.

The following sources and studies reveal more alarming facts about social isolation:

- **One in four Americans lives alone** according to the US Census Bureau, a 10 percent increase over the past decade. (Health Resources and Services Administration, January 2019.)
- **Social isolation is a growing health epidemic.** (Cigna Study, May 2018.)
- **The number of Americans with no close friends has tripled since 1985.** (*National Science Foundation Report,* 2014.)
- **Loneliness has become a public health hazard.** (Amy Ellis Nutt, "Loneliness Grows from Individual Ache to Public Health Hazard," *Washington Post,* January 31, 2016.)
- **Socially isolated people are twice as likely to die prematurely than more socially engaged people. Being socially isolated can shorten your life as much as being obese or smoking.** "Data across 308,849 individuals, followed for an average of 7.5 years, indicate that individuals with adequate social relationships have a 50 percent greater likelihood of survival compared to those with poor or insufficient social relationships." (Holt-Lunstad, Smith, and Layton, "Social Relationships and Mortality Risk: A Meta-analytic Review," 2010, PLoS Medicine , 7(7), e1000316.)
- **Socially isolated patients in hospitals (without family) are increasing as a symptom of an epidemic of social isolation.** (Dhruv Khullar, "How

Social Isolation Is Killing Us," *New York Times,* December 22, 2016.)

- **Loneliness and social isolation are risk factors for coronary heart disease and stroke.** (British Cardiology Society, 2016.)

- **Lonely individuals are more affected by negative interactions with others.** "Lonely individuals seek to fulfill unmet needs but generally are less forgiving of minor hassles and transgressions than nonlonely individuals." (Cacioppo, Norris, Decety, Monteleone, Nusbaum, "In the Eye of the Beholder: Individual Differences in Perceived Social Isolation Predict Regional Brain Activation to Social Stimuli," January 21, 2009, PMC, NIH.)

- **Socially isolated seniors are more likely to develop Alzheimer's.** (Alzheimer's Association, 2016.)

- **Socially isolated children and teens are more likely to develop heart disease twenty years later.** (Caspi, Harrington, Moffitt, et al., "Socially Isolated Children 20 Years Later," Archives of Pediatric and Adolescent Medicine, August, 2006.)

Distracted and Fragmented Conversations

It wasn't only my friend Becky who had disappeared from my life. Something else had disappeared, though I couldn't quite name it, leaving behind a strange sense of uncertainty, a lack of commitment, hurriedness, distraction, and even flakiness that plagued my interactions with others. For some reason, my connections just didn't feel solid anymore. It seemed I was bothering people when I phoned to chat, always a "bad time," as they were not only busy but completely absorbed in their own daily lives. I felt peripheral and nonessential to people I loved dearly—how did I fit in anymore, let alone compete with the exciting things in which people were immersed? Indeed, the instantly seductive immersions of our digital age (checking posts on our

Instagram app or bingeing on streamed episodes of *Outlander*) could keep our loved ones from returning a call even on a Sunday afternoon.

I couldn't figure out what the new normal of our digital age required for communicating, whatever the etiquette was or what the rules were for having good, old-fashioned heart-to-heart conversations. I never got the memo; I lamented that having long, thoughtful conversations had become outdated, like warm, cozy pastimes such as a quilting bee or teatime, comforts from the past. Even spontaneous conversations seemed to quickly fizzle out. At work, my coworkers didn't want to discuss anything in a face-to-face conversation, even though our desks were in the same room. They preferred emails, though we were only four feet apart!

Was I missing something? Why did I feel like an idiot for trying to rev up real conversations—at least conversations that lasted longer than two minutes? Or was it just me—people didn't want to talk to *me*? Whatever the case, I figured I needed to shut up and get with the program—spend more time on social media. Can't beat 'em, join 'em. Do more Facebook posts, tweeting, texting, messaging, emailing, emoji-sending, Instagram photos, and always, *always* the less said the better. Keep it smart, short, and "likable." And when no one is interested in chatting with you at the bar or lunch counter or even at a meetup, there's always your smartphone for company.

I resorted to social media more over the next two years, following people I knew online, including Becky, who appeared to be doing brilliantly on Facebook—even her daughter looked happy in her photos. She didn't accept my friend request and I cried for two days. Dare I ever call her again? I had left her at least a dozen messages by now.

I found comfort by watching more Netflix, drinking chardonnay, and having my fortune told by a lively variety of YouTube tarot readers. I lived by watching screens. I fended off my loneliness with screens—HD screens, smartphone screens, iPad screens, big movie theater screens. Screens for companionship, screens for belonging, screens for forgetting that no one had showed up at the hospital after my surgery. Screens to fill the emptiness of not having heart-to-heart conversations anymore.

Heart-to-hearts didn't only mean deep conversations, but also leisurely chats while lounging on a beach or long, meandering walks with a friend through the woods, dinner parties that lasted to midnight, sitting on a dock with fellow travelers watching sailboats come and go. A loving, forgiving hug after a misunderstanding. Just watching stupid movies together on a rainy afternoon.

Lost in my memories, I hardly noticed a pair of chickadees singing from the pine tree near my window. I stepped away from my laptop and sat in my wicker chair by the window for a closer view of the chickadees hopping from branch to branch. They seemed to be engaged in lively bird chatter—taking turns "telling it like it is." It suddenly struck me that I missed talking like those feisty little chickadees—*that's* what was causing me to feel so lonely! I could count on one hand the times I'd enjoyed free-spirited, heart-to-heart talks. It was truly liberating for me to name this thing that had haunted me for three years.

Becky loved chickadees. We had heart-to-hearts every week when I'd first moved to Maine seventeen years ago, sitting in her gazebo in her backyard full of lavender butterfly bushes. I still missed her. It had been three damn years since the last time we spoke.

I turned again to the window to watch the chickadees. One flew close to me on the nearest branch of the pine tree and stared at me, cocking his head and singing at the top of his tiny lungs. I listened, smiling, dazzled by his bold audacity. He was so full of himself! How wonderful, I thought, to be so full of it! For some reason, he had popped right by my windowsill to sing for me.

Suddenly, without thinking, without hesitation, I picked up my mobile and called Becky.

She answered! I greeted her by saying the chickadees had told me to call.

She laughed! Right away Becky said she was glad I called. I was shocked to hear she had recently suffered a moderate stroke and was slowly recovering. The normal routines in her life had been derailed, forcing her to quit her job. Her stepdaughter was in recovery from her opioid addiction and living with her. But Becky was overwhelmed with the needs of others as well as her own, and admitted it was time to reach out to her friends again.

She explained, "I can't concentrate anymore. In fact, I can't do very much of anything these days. I can't keep my balance well enough to take care of my family the way I want to, but Val, thank God for my friends. I'm so glad you called. I am so, *so* sorry I wasn't a good friend to you. I couldn't be there for you—I just couldn't face it and I hid away. It was wrong."

"You were going through something horrible, Becky."

We had a tearful heart-to-heart over the phone, and in two weeks, I circled back to Maine from Boston for a visit with her. Becky's stroke had slightly slowed down her speech and memory, but she still loved to talk. We sat in her gazebo in the garden taking long pauses to watch the cardinals, the finches, and the chickadees stopping at her bird feeder. All was forgiven with our promise to one another: "Let's not shy away again."

Isolation and Social Media: A Downward Spiral

I've wondered how many people have "shied away" or almost given up having heart-to-heart conversations with loved ones, let alone friends. I've often heard people over fifty admit how much they miss the "good old days" when taking a whole afternoon or evening to gab with friends or family members was essential to our sense of belonging in the world. But what happens to our sense of belonging when we're lucky to get fifteen minutes into a conversation without a distraction or interruption from our devices?

I resorted to reading social science research to find out if conversation was actually disappearing in our digital age. Sherry Turkle, a social science professor at Massachusetts Institute of Technology, has devoted the past twelve years to examining how our digital age is diminishing our time, focus, and appreciation for meaningful conversations. In her latest book, *Reclaiming Conversation: The Power of Talk in a Digital Age* (Penguin, 2016) she laments that when we check our phones while interacting with someone, then "what you lose is what a friend, teacher, parent, lover, or co-worker just said, meant, felt."

Sherry Turkle makes a compelling case that we can set good examples for our children, our peers, coworkers, and friends when we protect the time we need for face-to-face interactions. I've been heartened by her studies and her recommendations for ways to keep conversations vital in our lives. Many of us might not need social science research to convince ourselves that we need to reclaim conversation in these times, but after several years of feeling shunned, shut out, and dismissed, I've found her research downright reassuring, healing, and confidence-building.

Turkle's books and dozens of other studies I've read show us how social media can threaten our time for or interest in face-to-face conversation. Relying too much on social media and online social networks for a sense of connectedness can backfire, robbing us of the communication skills we need for talking about more important or difficult subjects. On the other hand, the proper, *balanced* use of social media and online networks can strengthen human bonds by helping us find social groups for connection, giving us access to more face-to-face opportunities to talk. Unfortunately, the research shows that if you are *already* lonely or isolated in your life, you are more likely to rely on social media too much and increasingly avoid conversation and meaningful face-to-face activities.

And when children and teens are feeling isolated, they are even more vulnerable. The American Academy of Pediatrics (AAP) warns parents about excessive use of social media using the phrase "Facebook depression" that may worsen as the child's brain develops.

A powerful phenomenon has grown out of our dependency on social media called FOMO, fear of missing out. This syndrome can cause depression as well as anxiety—particularly social anxiety. (Interestingly, long before the advent of social media, the term, FOMO, was coined in 2004, by author Patrick McGinnis, making his op-ed popular in an article in the magazine of the Harvard Business School.)

FOMO, fear of missing out, sums up the ways social media isolates us by keeping us constantly hooked:

- Checking our phones so we don't miss anyone trying to reach us.
- Checking out other people's lifestyles and comparing ourselves.
- Checking out the very latest updates on news, events, changes in plans.
- Checking our phones so we don't get left behind and forgotten.

Ironically, the harder we try to stay connected, the more isolated we become. These figures grabbed my attention:

- **Millennials who describe themselves as lonely report relying more on social media and online connections for companionship.** ("Social Media Use and Perceived Social Isolation Among Young Adults in the US," *Journal of Preventative Medicine,* 2017.)
- **Eighty-two percent of people believe that smartphone use at social gatherings actually hurts conversations.** (Tchiki Davis, PhD, Research and Development Consultant, Contributor to Greater Good Science Center's Science of Happiness course and blog.)

- **Some 92 percent of US adults now have a cellphone of some kind, and 90 percent of those cell owners say that their phone is frequently with them. Some 31 percent of cell owners say they never turn off their phone, and 45 percent say they rarely turn it off.** (Pew Research Center Study of 3,042 Americans, 2015.)

- **Women are more likely than men to feel cell use at social gatherings hurts the group:** 41 percent of women say it frequently hurts the gathering versus 32 percent of men who say the same. **Similarly, those over age fifty (45 percent) are more likely than younger cell owners (29 percent) to feel that cellphone use frequently hurts group conversations.** (Pew Research Center Study of 3,042 Americans, 2015.)

- **Only about half of Americans** (53 percent) have meaningful in-person social interactions, such as having an extended conversation with a friend or spending quality time with family, on a daily basis. (Cigna study, 2018.)

- **Facebook can make us feel lonely.** (Facebook Use Predicts Declines in Subjective Well-Being in Young Adults, University of Michigan Study, August 2013.)

- **Social media use alone is not a predictor of loneliness;** respondents defined as very heavy users of social media have a loneliness score (43.5) that is not markedly different from the score of those who never use social media (41.7). (Cigna study, 2018)

My big takeaway: When we feel left out of face-to-face connections (lonely) in our lives, we are more likely to turn to online connections as our sole source for companionship, which can lead to more social isolation and then to poor health, mentally as well as physically. It truly is a downward spiral.

I've created a diagram to illustrate my own ordeal of falling into a downward spiral of isolation after Becky failed to show up at the hospital and disappeared from my life. Social media was a comfort at first, but it drew me into more isolation and paralysis.

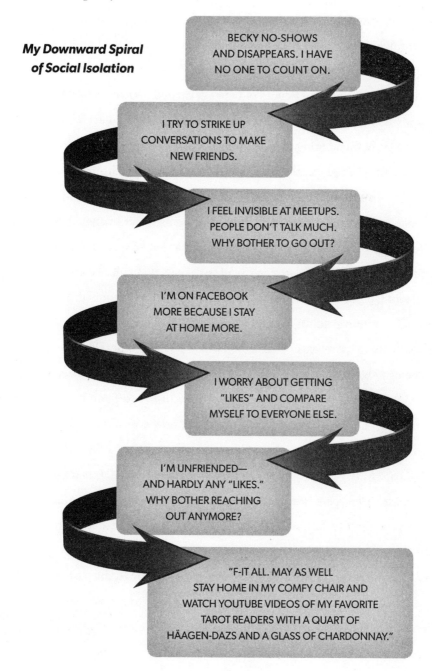

*My Downward Spiral
of Social Isolation*

BECKY NO-SHOWS AND DISAPPEARS. I HAVE NO ONE TO COUNT ON.

I TRY TO STRIKE UP CONVERSATIONS TO MAKE NEW FRIENDS.

I FEEL INVISIBLE AT MEETUPS. PEOPLE DON'T TALK MUCH. WHY BOTHER TO GO OUT?

I'M ON FACEBOOK MORE BECAUSE I STAY AT HOME MORE.

I WORRY ABOUT GETTING "LIKES" AND COMPARE MYSELF TO EVERYONE ELSE.

I'M UNFRIENDED— AND HARDLY ANY "LIKES." WHY BOTHER REACHING OUT ANYMORE?

"F-IT ALL. MAY AS WELL STAY HOME IN MY COMFY CHAIR AND WATCH YOUTUBE VIDEOS OF MY FAVORITE TAROT READERS WITH A QUART OF HÄAGEN-DAZS AND A GLASS OF CHARDONNAY."

The Pitfalls of Comparing Ourselves

In all the research about the ways social media can isolate us, there is a big elephant standing in the room of every study. That big, lurking creature is our deeply human fear of being judged by others. Social scientists have named this fear the "social evaluative threat." This term perfectly sums up the anxiety-provoking experiences of being evaluated and compared to certain standards of human achievement or normalcy. The social evaluative threat can be truly threatening for us at times, and it can be toxically stressful for our health—our physical health as well as our mental health.

The social evaluative threat is the reason so many of us are afraid of public speaking. Even extroverts avoid certain audiences. But imagine if *all* social situations evoked that same level of anxiety that public speaking does? Social scientists are noting an alarming rise of social anxiety in more common social situations, particularly where face-to-face conversation is required. Millennials and Generation Z adults are reporting higher levels of anxiety at face-to-face social activities, even casual situations where people simply chat. The anxiety of being judged by others is so painful that it keeps many of us isolated.

One social psychology professor from San Diego State University in California, Dr. Jean Twenge, has studied just how stressful it is for us to be sized up and compared to others. She is the author of *iGen: Why Today's Super-Connected Kids Are Growing Up Less Rebellious, More Tolerant, Less Happy—and Completely Unprepared for Adulthood—and What That Means for the Rest of Us.*

According to her studies and those of other researchers, the stress hormones called *catecholamines* skyrocket in our bodies when we feel judged, and the levels of catecholamines have been increasing in the past few years, particularly with millennials and Generation Z age groups. We don't need to have a diagnosis of social anxiety disorder to feel the effects of this rush of stress hormones. Many of us fear being judged when we are lacking in social status or coping with a stigmatized issue (addiction, unemployment, mental illness.) We would rather isolate ourselves than expose ourselves to people who might look down on us. We shy away from going out to socialize, let alone competing with others when we think we don't measure up. It's not just a matter of lacking self-esteem or confidence. And it's not just a matter of self-improvement because, no matter what we do, we live in a world that relentlessly measures us—our actions, our vocabulary, our clothing, our manners, our cars, our spending habits, the tone of our voice, even our facial expressions. Hopefully, amid all that judgment, we're brave enough to reach out and meet someone who genuinely likes us just as we are.

Social media increases the social evaluative threat to a whole new level of stress, which can be unbearable at times. Social media can make us feel we are being watched and scrutinized as if we're in a giant fishbowl. We ruthlessly compare ourselves and meticulously make sure we look good and send the right message. We protect and double-check our brand, our image, our every word. We tweak, delete, punctuate with emojis, enhance the lighting and colors, Photoshop, crop, and edit ourselves into oblivion. We can pick from handy menus what to say so it fits the criteria in the boxes for content. Multitudes of people on dating apps or hiring apps will swipe through all that hard work in seconds. And God forbid we mess up and the whole wide world can see it! Or someone who hates us wants to expose our past photos or records for our employers, lenders, or new partners to see. Nothing is sacred and nothing is safe. This is a hard world to be soft in, real in, human in.

We've learned the hard way that we must uphold the rules of social media: Be careful, smart, and crafty. Know what you're getting into. Don't be too spontaneous, too original, too deep, too intense, too honest—too *much*! Conversely, don't bother to put just any old, boring stuff out there if it's not too interesting for folks to see. So, we censor sharing the unplanned, unexpected, boring-but-happy moments that make us feel human. In short, the culture of social media doesn't appreciate the fine art of hanging out and being a little goofy. But in our *off*screen lives, we need those warm, relaxing nooks and crannies of our days to gather together, out of the spotlight, and into the magic of the moment. We need a break from being "on" all the time.

Based on social science research about social media as well as my own hard-won observations, the social evaluative threat plays on three common causes of human suffering: stigma, status, and shame. I call these the three Ss. They're isolating forces that lure us into comparing ourselves with others and drive up our stress hormones when we feel judged.

If we're suffering from a highly stigmatized issue (addiction, mental illness) or our status is different than others (being broke, unemployed) or we're feeling a sense of shame or defectiveness, then we're more vulnerable to anxiety and avoidance of others. And then, according to researchers, we're more vulnerable to isolation and using social media for companionship—and the spiral deepens ever more viciously as we crave the social media that makes us even more isolated.

When we are going through an isolating period, it might be helpful to check in with ourselves to spot if any of the three Ss are making us feel lonely.

Stigma: We're isolated because it's not okay to talk about our issue in most social situations. We must keep it secret and hidden.

Status: We're isolated because we've gotten the message that we're inferior to others. (Even if we don't believe we're inferior, we might be dealing with groups of people who judge us as inferior—or invisible.)

Shame: We believe something is wrong with us. Shame is often the result of internalized beliefs stemming from societal forces of stigma and inferior status.

I've created a short self-assessment to explore the forces in our lives, internally and externally, that might be keeping us isolated.

What Isolates You: A Self-Assessment

For questions 1–4, choose the statement that best describes you.

1. **The Social Evaluative Threat (How much does social judgment affect you?)**

   a. I don't go to social events, period—way too much pressure.

   b. I'm very sensitive to being judged by others and must pick situations carefully where I feel comfortable.

   c. I sometimes feel uncomfortable, but I usually get out for social events.

   d. Social judgment doesn't bother me too much. I don't let what other people think of me get in the way of having a great time.

2. **Social Stigma**

   a. I'm dealing with an issue that I can't talk about with anyone.

   b. I'm dealing with an issue that I can only share with one or two people—otherwise, it's a topic I don't discuss.

   c. I have an issue that is hard to talk about with most people, but I've found a supportive group of people where it's okay to talk about it.

   d. I don't have issues that I need to hide in my life now. I share almost anything.

3. **Social Status—Comparing Ourselves**

   a. I am facing issues that make me feel inferior to others. I lack what most of my peers have.

b. I feel inferior to others in certain social situations, but I do have some friends and colleagues who totally accept me as I am.

c. I usually don't feel inferior to others. It really doesn't bother me most of the time how other people live. (But yeah, every now and then I get a bit envious!)

d. I'm very content with what I have and what I've achieved.

4. Shame and Low Self-Worth

a. My feelings of not being worthy frequently bother me.

b. Thankfully, I feel, at least sometimes, that, I have a lot to offer others. But I can still feel bad about myself more often than I'd like.

c. I am a fairly confident person and feel good about myself most of the time.

d. Fortunately, I'm very accepting of myself and feel that I am a good, trustworthy person who has much to offer others.

If you answered mostly As or Bs, you are more likely to be stressed and anxious in social situations in your community. You might benefit from having a safe, nonjudging, accepting person to help you (confidante, therapist, coach) in addition to, or prior to, venturing out to social events. You might also benefit from a support group or a group of like-minded people to boost your confidence. If you answered mostly Cs and Ds, it's probably easier for you to get out to meetups and social events without too much stress and anxiety.

5. Survival Mode
Social, Economic, and Cultural Barriers That Can Isolate Us

Check any of the following barriers that make it difficult to build social networks in person.

Chronic or serious illness or chronic pain (physical or mental illnesses or both)

Disability (visual, hearing, mobility, brain injury, developmental, other)

Being the primary caregiver without support

Lack of income

Working too many hours (to make ends meet)

Working weekends or overnights (and missing out on social opportunities)

Living alone

Lack of transportation or transportation limitations

Loss of your home, frequently changing homes, or homelessness

Surviving a natural disaster

Living in a rural area and feeling "cut off" from social events

Living in an unsafe neighborhood, fearful of going out at night

Depression

Feeling shame and low self-worth

Social anxiety

Addiction and recovery

Grief, recovering from the death of a loved one

Divorce or break-up

Empty nest situation (Now that the kids are gone, you are struggling to build new social networks.)

Retirement (Now that you don't work, you are struggling to find new friends.)

Major promotion or enormously successful milestone in your life that your friends or family members cannot relate to or feel threatened by—they think you'll leave them behind. Big success can be isolating for some of us. Even college students leaving family members who never went to college can feel isolated.

Being exceptionally talented or gifted (People often cannot talk about this topic of outshining others, so we hide this aspect of ourselves and feel lonely and "different." Our abilities can be threatening to others.)

Other: Please add your own barrier if needed.

If you checked several situations in the list on the previous page, it's plain to see you are in survival mode with a lot on your plate. Please be compassionate, patient, and understanding with yourself while you face the forces that isolate you.

It is more important to nurture our self-compassion and patience than to rush to "get out there" and meet the right people all at once. It will take a lot of time and a good amount of focus to build a support system, but please don't give up. It took me six years to build a thriving social network in Boston after I moved from Maine in 2012, without friends, without family, broke, and exhausted from a chronic illness. Scraping by to pay my rent (no small feat in Boston) and working ridiculous hours imprisoned me in survival mode.

When it comes right down to it, survival mode is isolating. Period.

Little by little, with small acts of kindness for ourselves, we can understand how the demands of survival mode, stigma, and shame have gripped us in isolation. As we grasp what is keeping us isolated, hopefully we can befriend our loneliness and not feel ashamed of it. We can learn from our loneliness, listen to it, let it call us into action.

Despite the forces of survival mode, plus the stigma and shame we face, people have broken through isolation and created communities of acceptance and belonging. I've witnessed this resilience and resourcefulness with the clients I served as a rehabilitation counselor and as a friend and colleague. I've known marginalized, abandoned, and painfully isolated people who never quite gave up and found their people. It's a daunting task for most of us.

Part Two is devoted to this brave, exhausting, but enormously rewarding task of breaking through isolation and discovering our people.

Let's befriend our loneliness as we befriend our communities.

Breaking Through Isolation

• • • •

CHAPTER THREE

What It Takes to Break through Isolation

Daring to Chat

One year after landing in Boston and settling in, I assessed my progress in building a social life in my new city. Unfortunately, I was still alone most of the time. Aside from a couple of acquaintances, I didn't have any new friends in Boston. It was tempting to slip into a sense of failure, more loneliness, and pining for the friends I hadn't (yet) made.

At least, as a consolation prize to give myself, I was grateful for my three breakthroughs that had kept me from giving up and giving in to isolation. I could acknowledge how brave I had been those few times I had dared to chat with people. I had taken the risk of being ignored, snubbed, or pushed away. What had sparked my courage to take those risks?

I concluded that genuinely caring for others had given me courage to reach out. To further boost my courage, my insatiable curiosity had been a driving force for pushing through isolation. In short, the combined qualities of caring and curiosity pulled me through awkward moments of reaching out to others.

Here are my hard-won revelations I cherished as my consolation prize for surviving my lonely first year in Boston:

1. **Caring and showing up for others was sometimes well worth the risk.** My experience with my coworker, Pat, on the days after the Boston Marathon Bombing, had taught me the power of caring and showing up, even though I didn't feel strong, worthy, or confident. Pat and I didn't get along at work, but the ice had been broken between us. I had taken the risk of reaching out to her on that day I had seen her in distress at her desk. I had asked if she was okay, knowing that she could easily have pushed me away or ignored my offer of caring. But she didn't—she welcomed my interest in her. Taking that risk of reaching out was not only worth it, but it broke me out of my isolation and fear.

2. **My caring for others gave me the courage I needed to take risks.** My breakthrough with Pat gave me the courage to reach out to my old friend, Becky, back in Maine, after she had disappeared from my life for three years. The glorious experience of reuniting with her confirmed that the courage I had mustered up was vital to saving our friendship. (I should also give a shout out to the bold singing chickadee by my window who beckoned me to conjure up my courage!)

3. **My curiosity and interest in my new community got me off the couch and out the door.** I have a story to tell about a magical day when I followed my curiosity.

One sunny, brisk October Saturday, I took off on an adventure to explore the historic town of Concord, Massachusetts, and Walden Pond. Concord was the home of Henry David Thoreau, a great influencer in my life. His most famous work, *Walden: Or, Life in the Woods*, had been my bible since the age of seventeen and had encouraged my love of quiet, watery places and long, solitary walks.

After my reverent walk at the sanctuary of Walden Pond, starving for lunch, I found a cozy café on Main Street in Concord. At the bar, I ordered a bowl of butternut squash soup. A side dish of soft, warm cornbread hit the spot while I waited for the soup to cool. To the right of me, a woman about my age was reading a brochure about Thoreau's famous home, a prime tourist attraction in Concord.

I started to say hello to this woman as she quietly read her brochure, but I hesitated for a moment. Maybe I shouldn't interrupt her. Maybe I would appear too friendly or lonely. As I sipped my soup, I played and replayed scenarios in my mind about what might happen if I said hello to her. I could say hello and she might only reply with a quick "Hi," and go right back to her reading. Or perhaps I could say hello and tell her I was interested in Henry David Thoreau and Walden Pond. Or I could say hello and she might welcome my greeting and ask me something.

Or I would not say hello at all and mind my own business.

I finished my soup and gazed toward the front windows of the café, pausing to enjoy the streaming rays of sunshine across the happy lunch crowd chatting at their tables.

When I turned back to the bar, the woman next me looked at me and shyly smiled.

Thinking I had nothing to lose by saying hello, I offered my greeting. "Hi, this place is great, isn't it?"

"I love it here," she answered. "I come here on Saturdays when I volunteer in Concord."

"Where?" I was eager to know.

"At Henry David Thoreau's home. I'm a docent there."

"Oh, that's wonderful. I've been reading his work since I was seventeen. I'd like to visit his home someday."

"I'd be happy to give you a tour sometime on a Saturday."

"I would like that very much—thanks so much. Do you work anywhere else on the weekdays?"

"Yes, I'm a social worker at Mass General Hospital. I live in Arlington, halfway between Boston and Concord, so I spend my weekends volunteering here and taking nature photos at Walden Pond. At Thoreau's home they sell my Walden Pond cards and calendars."

"I would love to see your photography sometime," I eagerly replied.

I could tell she perked up when she talked about Walden Pond. It heartened me that she so freely talked about her passions—and she loved chatting! I was relieved that she eagerly shared her interests in photography, her volunteering, her love of Thoreau and his writings. Then I suddenly remembered I hadn't even asked her name.

"Oh, my goodness, sorry, I forgot to ask your name!"

She chuckled. "Barbara. Barbara Olson. And yours?"

"Val Walker."

Her accent didn't seem Bostonian. Mid-Atlantic, Midwest maybe? "Where are you from?"

"Michigan. I moved here twenty-six years ago. And Concord is my true 'happy place,' as they say. I've made so many friends here and met people from all around the world by volunteering at Thoreau's home."

"That's brilliant—the way you've met so many friends by volunteering. It sounds as if, for a person transplanted here from Michigan, that your interest in Thoreau has helped you bring other like-minded people into your life."

"Yes, that's true." She studied me for a moment and remarked, "You sound like you're a transplant, too."

"You're right, originally from Virginia, and then Maine, and a year ago I moved to the Boston area. I live in Woburn."

Our conversation flowed easily, and in just thirty minutes, Barbara had invited me to a tour of Thoreau's home as well as a Christmas party at her home. Thrilled and amazed, I realized this was the first time in two years that anyone had invited me to an honest-to-God, real *party*! Finally, I felt normal, accepted, likable. Yes, when it came right down to healing my isolation, there was nothing as reassuring as a friendly invitation. My encounter with Barbara led to more invitations and gatherings. In particular, one event opened my eyes to a whole new world of opportunities.

Barbara and her boyfriend hosted a springtime party that featured a storytelling marathon. They named this the Moth Hour Party after the famous National Public Radio show. Guests were invited to tell a five-minute story about any true-life event they wanted to share. We could choose an amusing personal story, poignant or light, to offer to an appreciative audience of fellow storytellers.

At this lively event on a warm May afternoon, I heard a dozen thoughtful and touching stories from Barbara's guests. This storytelling event invoked everyone's playfulness, sense of adventure, and curiosity in others—a true social mixer. I had never witnessed such a successful ice-breaker for a crowd of colleagues and friends. In story after story, alongside breaks for plentiful food and drink, people of all ages told their five-minute tales of misadventures, discoveries, revelations, and lessons well-learned.

I happily shared a funny story of falling in love with a boy in the sixth grade, believing he had psychic powers and could read my mind. (As a twelve-year old, I was fascinated with everything psychic—ESP, astrology, telepathy, and Ouija boards.) I was convinced this boy psychically "had my number."

Telling my quirky little story allowed me to share my long-dormant playfulness and sense of humor. I finally enjoyed myself at a party—for the first time in seven years! Indeed, I had forgotten how wonderful it felt to share a burst of joy and laughter with a group of people. It had been far too long since I'd felt this relaxed and open at a social event.

Thankfully, by following my curiosity and saying hello to Barbara at the café in Concord on that October afternoon, I had sparked a new friendship as well as a chance to make other friends.

A Safe Space

As I savored the warmth and sense of belonging at Barbara's storytelling party, I had another breakthrough revelation: I needed a safe space to open up with others. Barbara, a warm and welcoming host, had created a safe space that put people at ease. She made us all feel so welcome and comfortable that even the shyest among us could bravely share our stories. Of course, she was also a professional social worker, but still, she rocked a good party.

It occurred to me that most of us who have been isolated for a long period need a safe person or safe space to *begin* reaching out. If we are struggling through an isolating experience such as an illness, loss of a job, or a breakup with a partner, we might hesitate to reach out or to bother to chat at all. But in certain safe situations, amazingly, we could step out of our fear of judgment and truly connect in a fulfilling, meaningful, and maybe even joyous way.

As a former rehabilitation counselor and case manager for twenty-two years, I've marveled at how people could recover from social anxiety and years of hiding and shame by joining forces with one safe person or safe group. Indeed, having one safe person with whom we could confide our deep loneliness was the only way to begin our breakthrough out of isolation. I often accompanied my individual clients to their first social meetups or first twelve-step groups or new jobs. They needed someone to go out with them into their communities "for moral support," as they ventured "out there" to build social networks. Of course, they were petrified. My clients usually needed several social outings with me before they were ready to go solo and function on their own.

But it struck me that I, *too*, needed someone safe and accepting to go out with or at least a safe group I could go to—warm, welcoming, and accepting. Of course, I couldn't rely only on my new friend Barbara for all my support. It was essential I had a regular safe space for me, a foundation of support.

I examined why I had not done more to find a therapist or support group my first year in Boston without friends. Perhaps I might have been less lonely (before my encounter with Barbara) if I had turned to a therapist or support group much sooner. Why had I *not* done that? I had been a counselor for twenty-two years, so why did I not think to try harder to find that safe support I so dearly needed?

I had some answers (or maybe excuses):

- Therapists or support groups might *not* feel safe to me.
- It was too much trouble to hunt for the right therapist or support group.
- I feared I could not afford a therapist and didn't want to get bogged down in scheduled appointments and keeping up with payments.
- I didn't want to fight Boston traffic to get to a support group or therapist.
- My crazy, unpredictable work schedule didn't allow the time.
- I was too darn tired and in too much pain because of my chronic illness with colitis.

These were the reasons I didn't bother to get to a therapist or attend a support group. Yes, I'd chosen instead to try to make new friends the old-fashioned way, by just chatting with people who appeared friendly. But that was just not enough.

Fortunately, at one of Barbara's parties, I met someone who was going to a support group for chronic illness. My encounter with her was the perfect nudge I needed to finally go to a support group for colitis. Oddly, I have my chronic illness to thank for leading me to a wonderful support group for people with IBD (inflammatory bowel disease.)

Dealing with the embarrassing and anxiety-provoking problems of running frequently to the bathroom was a common theme with my IBD support cronies. It was clear many of us were socially isolated during the worst of our flare-ups, struggling with what was unpredictable, painful, exhausting, and humiliating. The problems with our bowels interfered with our romantic aspirations, to say the least, let alone any intimate get-togethers with friends and families. My support group cronies cheered me when I shared my modest victories of trying social meetups despite my "disappearing acts" of hiding in the bathroom for fifteen minutes at a time. Many members of the group were similarly plagued by the awkward interactions of colitis and social anxiety, which played off each other mercilessly—but, thankfully, we had one another and we all "got it." Being heard, understood, and supported was crucial to our recovery from the isolation of our illness.

In a well-organized support group, participants tackle the stigma, status, and shame (the three Ss) that have kept us isolated. Our stories, shared in a safe space, not only reveal what is keeping us isolated, but they help us learn from one another and explore ways to cope.

Support groups can be a brilliant way to meet new people and regain our social confidence for connecting face to face. But some of us might prefer more privacy with just one individual person we trust. If we are fortunate enough to have someone in our own circle already with whom we can turn for comfort and understanding, we may be able to recover from our isolating experiences more easily. However, if we lack such a person in our own natural support system, it might be best to find a psychotherapist, chaplain, coach, or mentor. It makes a huge difference having someone to talk to about how lonely we feel.

Isolation is not something we can heal without another human being. Breaking out of isolation is not a task we can accomplish simply with the aid of our devices, even though they can help us locate the people and resources we need. Breaking out of isolation requires more than relying on the comfort of our beloved animal companions, though their presence is also vital to our healing. If we are truly isolated, we need to be with a person *in person* or at least with a real listener on the phone.

But here's the catch: What if we don't have a safe person to talk to? Who do we call? What do we do?

Where do we *begin*?

One of the best ways to begin is to turn to a helpline, hotline, or crisis line. I can't emphasize enough how vital it is to have a caring voice on that helpline. Most of these helplines are connected to suicide prevention hotlines and emotional support lines, but we don't need to be suicidal or in a crisis to "qualify" for time talking with a warm, caring (and trained) listener. Being lonely or lacking social support is a perfectly good reason to call.

Every state has support lines, many of which can be accessed by calling the United Way in our cities, often reached by dialing 2-1-1 or three-digit numbers—set up similarly to 9-1-1 systems. (Or go to www.211.org or the United Way website for your city or town.) Here in Boston, my call to the 2-1-1 helpline guided me to their "Call to Talk" warmline. Any lonely or isolated person can call just to talk, every day if needed.

Even if we have no one to turn to, we can begin by calling a helpline or mental health support line or by calling a counseling center directly for a referral. We can also reach out to a church, synagogue, or religious organization and ask for pastoral counseling services for support. We don't need to worry if we don't have enough information to locate a person or group to talk to because most counseling services, ministries, schools, or medical centers provide referrals for support or have social workers at hand to help us. (You can read more about how to find and utilize helplines, hotlines, counseling services, and other community supports in Chapter Four.)

When it comes right down to it, we need to get "out of our heads" for healing our loneliness and, instead, turn to a person who listens without judgment. Even if we have our beloved animals beside us for comfort, as human beings we do, at some point, need genuine human contact. We are biologically hardwired for it and, come hell or high water, we all reach a breaking point when we have no choice but to turn to someone—voice-to-voice, face-to-face, hand-to-hand.

Knowing the Indicators of a Healthy Connection

Although we may know very well how important it is to have a person to talk to or to have a confidante, we still might be reluctant to trust someone. We just don't know how to be certain about who is safe, trustworthy, or worth our while. And worse, we may have recently lost a supportive, safe person in our lives and are grieving that sense of safety, belonging, and love.

As a rehabilitation counselor as well as a survivor of long bouts of isolation, I'd like to share what I've learned about the best "go to" people for supporting us. When we are looking for a safe space, a friend, a therapist, or a support group, it helps to be aware of the indicators of a healthy, safe connection.

First of all, if we feel vulnerable after a long period of isolation, it's most helpful to turn to a person (or support group) who possesses at least a couple of the following comforting qualities:

Empathy: Someone who can feel what we feel, even if he or she hasn't been through quite the same experience.

Warmth: Someone to smile, welcome us, and receive us. (And in some situations, a hug is a godsend or at least a good, solid handshake.)

Compassion: Someone who can understand and not judge us.

Patience: Someone who doesn't rush us to "get to the point" or "get over it."

Good listening skills: We need to be heard. Our listener offers eye-to-eye contact, without distractions or interruptions.

Respect: We need to feel worthy, with our human rights honored and upheld.

Reliability: Someone who keeps his or her commitments or promises (at least tries hard).

One way to reflect on what a comforting (safe) person or group means for us is to consider what Maya Angelou, the wise, brilliant author who once said: "I've learned that people will forget what you said, people will forget what you did, but people will never forget how you made them feel."

She's right. How do we make each other *feel*?

It might be helpful to think back on a time someone comforted you in the past few months, even if only a brief encounter. How did this comforting interaction make you feel?

Here are some common reactions to being comforted:

"I felt heard."

"I wasn't the only one going through this—I was not alone."

"I was more hopeful that I could move on."

"I felt loved and cared for."

"I finally mattered to someone."

"I felt calmer, more at peace with my situation."

"I felt empowered, stronger. I could believe in myself."

"I learned something from this. I had a breakthrough, a realization."

"I finally felt normal again."

In my work as a rehabilitation counselor, I frequently resorted to using a quick, helpful checklist of indicators of a healthy connection developed by the Jean Baker Miller Institute at Wellesley College in Wellesley, Massachusetts. Essentially, they created a handy checklist called "The Five Good Things." These five indicators of a good connection are the features of a "growth-fostering relationship," according to the Jean Baker Miller Institute. "The Five Good Things" is a handy tool for assessing what connections work best for us. These indicators are:

1. Zest
2. Worth
3. Knowledge
4. Initiative
5. Desire for more connection

In my own words, in a nutshell, I will describe what these indicators mean to me as well as to the clients I've served.

- **Zest: We feel energized by the interaction. We "light up" or "perk up."**
  Example: You feel a spark. You are jazzed when the host of the event warmly greets you and enthusiastically introduces you to her friends.
- **Worth: We sense that we are valued and appreciated.**
  Example: You feel heard and valued at a business meeting where everyone is given equal time to talk—and no one interrupts or dominates the conversation.

- **Knowledge: We can transparently exchange information, resources, or knowledge.**

  Example: At a meetup, your friends readily offer resources and tips when you've asked for suggestions for finding an Alzheimer's support group. And conversely, they welcome *your* suggestions to help them.

- **Initiative: We want to take action and move to the next step. We feel motivated.**

  Example: Your fellow sports fans watching the game at the bar invite you to come hear a band playing at the restaurant next Saturday. You are already making plans to be there.

- **Desire for more connection: We want to see the person or the group again.**

  Example: You had so much fun at the trivia night event last week that you are going to be a regular player every Tuesday.

An encounter with a person or a group might not match *all* five of these indicators, but even a couple of them are heartening signs that there is potential for a longer-lasting relationship. In other words: it's a *go*.

Of course, in the reverse, the opposite of these indicators reveals a less-than-healthy connection. Perhaps these are red flags that this might not be a good fit:

- ***Lack* of Zest:** We feel drained by the encounter. We are tired and even our brain feels zapped.

  Example: People hardly made eye contact with you at the party. You were invisible, faded into the woodwork, and felt empty rather than alive.

- ***Lack* of Worth:** We sense we weren't valued or appreciated.

  Example: At the job where you volunteer, your supervisor praised the hard work of others but did not mention how you had contributed.

- *Lack* of **Knowledge:** We feel confused or unclear about the information or the information is incomplete—we need to know more. We feel left out of the loop and "the last to know."

  Example: At a doctor visit you had several questions to ask, but the doctor was too rushed to answer more than the first two on your list.

- *Lack* of **Initiative:** We don't feel hopeful, inspired, or motivated.

  Example: You worked hard to make a nice cake for the break room at your office but hardly anyone had a piece. You are discouraged and won't bother to bring food again (and are trying not to be pissed off at your coworkers.)

- *Lack* of **Desire to Meet Again:** There is no interest in meeting again.

  Example: You've tried a few book club meetups, but you aren't so keen on the books being discussed. You just aren't into it anymore and won't come to the next meetup.

We all possess our own personal checklists for the "all-clear" in moving forward with a new relationship. We all have our red flags, our BS detectors, body language signals, trusting our gut, our "Spidey" sense, our radar.

But there's a fine line between using our checklists and jumping to conclusions too soon. In a deeper sense, there is an even finer line between being judgmental and being wise about who is "good" for us. Most of us tend to believe that finding "our people" or "our tribe" means finding only the *like-minded* people.

However, to my great surprise, I have found that some of my most loyal friends and colleagues *don't* share my beliefs or values (differing political or religious stances) and they are some of the kindest people I know. (Think about how a few of our senators who strongly disagreed with each other eventually became close friends, such as John McCain and Joe Biden.)

I have a couple of friends with whom I'd never have a deep conversation or dare reveal my political beliefs, but when things have been tough, I've relied on their generosity. They've helped me move my furniture out of my tiny apartment, schlepping boxes up and down three flights of stairs. If I was to reflect again on what Maya Angelou said—that it's how people make us *feel*, rather than how much we agree with them or not—then I would err on the side of the kindness of friends or even strangers. I can usually spot their genuine caring and consideration for others because that *always* makes me feel good.

But still, "reading" people can be tricky. People can surprise us. Nice people can do shitty things (the smiling, polite coworkers who roll their eyes when you talk), and the crabby folks (not too warm and fuzzy) turn out to be true-blue friends. Though it's helpful to have our checklists and know what we are looking for, sometimes people show up in the nick of time in our lives, without the bells and whistles of shared interests, values, or tastes—and they have your back!

Restoring Our Confidence in Conversation

After a long bout of isolation—say, recovering from cancer or grieving the death of a loved one—we might feel out of place during casual conversations or at social events. Our isolating experiences have interfered with keeping our social lives up to speed, and we feel awkward, even just chatting. Basically, we are feeling out of place because we are out of *practice* with talking. When we don't use certain muscle groups and don't keep ourselves conditioned, we get out of shape and lose our muscle tone. Similarly, this also happens with our conversational skills—we lose our *social* conditioning, our tone, and become "rusty" with our social skills. Chatting feels odd, unfamiliar, maybe even scary. Plus, chit chat may seem exhausting and tedious.

Perhaps we need a safe place to practice our conversational skills before braving social events in the wider community.

One of the many benefits for finding a safe space, a therapist, or a support group is that we can practice our conversational skills without judgment or social expectations. No one will rush us as we struggle to find our words or think out loud as we speak. It's okay to stutter, repeat ourselves, "go blank," or pronounce something incorrectly without judgment. Over time, week after week, month after month, we regain our confidence in being able to talk as well as listen, to read the social cues of when it's okay to say something or not. It's vital that we restore our confidence in using our conversational skills, so we are ready to brave social situations in the real world. In short, having a safe space to practice talking prepares us to "get out there."

Here in the Boston area, I've noticed a proliferation of meetups and other support groups for people with social anxiety. It has become okay to "out" ourselves as socially anxious people by going to these groups that accept and encourage us. There are meetups for social anxiety at cozy restaurants where young college students as well as seniors in their sixties gather to share pizza— and talk, ironically, about how hard it is to talk.

This growth in social anxiety groups is an indication of what social scientists such as Jean Twenge, PhD, and Sherry Turkle have told us: We are becoming increasingly more anxious with casual conversation and socializing offline. It's no surprise that groups for social anxiety are increasing around the country. Socially isolated people are the most sensitive to judgment (the social evaluative threat, according to social scientists). The surge in social anxiety meetups and support groups is a heartening sign that even the most isolated among us are "getting out there" to find "our people."

Over the years, working with people with autism and other developmental and intellectual disabilities, I've noticed an enormous increase in social skills coaching to address social anxiety. Teens and young adults are provided social skills training groups, coaching, and community activities to help build confidence in social situations. I currently teach workshops using theater games and teambuilding exercises for participants with intellectual disabilities to practice communication skills, problem-solving, and self-advocacy.

In recent years, I've observed innovative new trends for helping people break out of social isolation. It's become far more acceptable for people to go to supportive groups that are founded on the very issues that have isolated us—a chronic illness, addiction, social anxiety, unemployment, divorce, death, and loss. I've seen more meetups and groups for trauma survivors, abuse survivors, sexual assault survivors, as well as unemployment support groups, grief support groups, and others. It's encouraging, yet stunningly ironic, that many of us are building community around the very thing that has isolated us. At the very least, these groups help us start talking and break us through the ice that has kept us silent, powerless, and isolated.

Certainly, my chronic illness of colitis led me to a new community of fellow IBD survivors. I had the chance to tell my story and hear many others.

When it comes right down to it, telling our stories is one of the most powerful ways we can break out of isolation. I'm thrilled that so many meetups and other groups, online and offline, are inviting us to build a sense of belonging by sharing our stories.

Self-Advocacy: It's Not Just about Asking for Help

A useful skill for breaking out of isolation and seeking support is self-advocacy. *Advocacy* is the fine art of building support by showing people how they can make a real difference in our lives, not simply meeting our basic needs.

Ultimately, when we have an opportunity to tell our story and be heard, we automatically become our own self-advocate. We make a case for ourselves by showing others how we faced a challenge and did something about it. Stories are always about challenges, taking action, and getting results (for better or for worse.) Those who listen to our story have a sense of what issues we've been struggling with and how we've been coping. It's much easier for the listener to understand our needs and find a way to help us when they've been *shown* a viable and specific way to help us. In a sense, being self-advocates means we are presenting a situation and showing others *how* they can help.

When we need to ask for support from others, it helps to know how to self-advocate. Self-advocating usually entails briefly telling the listener our story by describing our situation—the challenges and how we are coping, *what already works for us*—and then inviting the listener to help in a specific way. In short, advocacy comes right down to making a pitch—making a good case for ourselves and inviting the person to chip in or join us in our mission. It's not just about *asking* for help. Instead, it's about *inviting* people to join us in a solution, a mission, a cause.

For example, if we are seeking help with finding friends after recently relocating to a new city, we can search tips, resources, or even hands-on help by making our pitches to those who have also relocated and would understand our challenges. Going to a newcomers' meetup or looking for newcomers' programs at community centers, schools, or places of worship can get us acquainted with people who might be most inclined to hear our pitch about what we are seeking. Fellow newcomers know the feelings of being unfamiliar in a new setting and the courage it takes to reach out for friendships and fellowships. (I even know friends who go to newcomers' meetups just to make new friends, even though they are no longer newcomers in their cities. It's a great way to meet people who are hungrier for making contact and expanding their support networks.)

And a quick suggestion: For networking of any kind, business or social, whether or not we have a job, it usually helps to have a calling card—it doesn't have to be a business card. Even a simple card with our name and contact info and a nice image or design is useful for making new friends.

Self-advocacy is a skill that is frequently misunderstood and confused with assertiveness. Instead of asking for what we *need* and finding a win-win solution (assertiveness), as self-advocates, we tell people about our *goal* and explore with others how they can participate in reaching that goal. In short, self-advocacy is a more proactive approach to building support because it focuses less on our needs and reassures others that we are in charge of taking care of ourselves. Indeed, self-advocacy is networking—networking to build community.

People are often willing to help us, but they just don't want to get "sucked in" to uncertain and unpredictable situations ("What am I getting into here?") However, when people know exactly how they can help by doing one specific thing (say, picking up our medications for two weeks when we are recovering from surgery), it is much easier for them to join in. And as long as people know we are taking care of ourselves with a useful strategy, they won't be scared away, fearing a "bottomless pit" of neediness and chaos. It's up to us, even if we have been lonely and isolated for a long period, to make it clear to others that we are in charge of our lives and not looking for people to save us.

Furthermore, one of the benefits of self-advocating is that we can create community with those people who have stepped up to help us. We can "return the favor" with those who've helped us by hosting gatherings with them, such as inviting them for a meal or party. It is essential that we offer our gratitude. Our gratitude is what builds community, especially with those who have been helpful to us. Most people like to help others because they want to make a difference and make others feel better. And best of all, we can offer to help others with *their* needs, particularly as we get to know them. It's amazing how contagious helping one another can be, and this reciprocity, along with great doses of gratitude (and love), is exactly what builds a strong community.

When we offer to help others and when we advocate for our own support, we are building solid connections where we have *each other's* backs.

CHAPTER FOUR

Turning to Our Community for Support

It Really Does Take a Village: The Networks That Support Us

Before we begin to find our pathways out of isolation, it's good to pause and take a big, wide look at the scope of support networks around us. To get the "lay of the land" and to navigate the land of social support, it's helpful to know that three decades ago, social scientists (James House, Thomas Wills, and others) categorized four distinct networks of support, in no particular order:

- **Emotional Support**

  People with whom we can confide and share our deepest thoughts and feelings.

- **Tangible Support (also known as Instrumental Support)**

  People who help us with hands-on, practical assistance (errands, caregiving, picking us up from the hospital).

- **Affiliative Support (also known as Companion Support)**

  People we meet in the wider community; groups we belong to (meetups, volunteering, classes, travel groups, colleagues, support groups, political campaigns, professional associations, clubs, and many others). Affiliations help to grow our sense of belonging.

- **Knowledge Support (also known as Informational Support)**

People who provide advice, information, skills, wisdom, resources, ideas. People who assist us in evaluating our actions (reality checks), help us make decisions, and plan our strategies. (Some social scientists believe there should be a fifth support network called **Esteem Support**, for people to help us evaluate ourselves, say, for getting feedback about ourselves, but I find it easier to include this support with our informational support network.)

I personally developed a diagram, on the facing page, showing how the four social support networks all overlap and provide us with many opportunities for building connections in our communities.

I like to think of the four social support networks as the "four food groups" that nourish our sense of belonging. Ideally, we can benefit from a healthy variety of nourishment from all four groups. We can foster a variety of friendships and fellowships, and it's better not to depend on just one person or group for *all* our needs. For example, if I look back to the years when I relied so much on my good friend Becky in Maine, I can understand why I was left high and dry when she disappeared after my surgery. It would have been easier if I had invested more time in developing other relationships, beyond the emotional support of just one or two friends. Essentially, we are better off not "putting all of our eggs in one basket" and keeping agile with a wider range of relationships (even if we are introverts.) In short, it takes a village to provide the support we need.

Elaine Cheung, PhD, a researcher at Northwestern University's Feinberg School of Medicine in Chicago says, "Too often people don't think about

Our Social Support Networks

EMOTIONAL SUPPORT
People We Confide In
Feeling Safe, Confidential,
Private, Empathic,
Good Listeners,
Meaningful Conversations,
We Can Be Vulnerable,
Acceptance, Respect,
Comfort

AFFILIATIVE SUPPORT
Groups We Join
Common Interests,
Common Causes,
Purposeful Activities,
Meaningful Activities,
Creative Activities,
Passions, Callings,
Recreation, Hobbies,
Fun Stuff

THE WIDER COMMUNITY
Helplines, Hotlines, Warmlines,
Support Groups,
Twelve-Step Groups,
Counseling, Coaching,
Meetups, Associations,
Clubs, Volunteering,
Serving Causes, Classes,
Study Groups, Travel,
Faith-Based Communities,
Advocacy, Social Action

TANGIBLE SUPPORT
People Who Assist Us
Hands-On Support,
Errands, Shopping,
Home Care, Cleaning,
Moving, Caregiver
Support, Transportation,
Assist with Doctor
Visits, Financial Aid,
Food Aid

KNOWLEDGE SUPPORT
People with Knowledge
People with Experience
(Have "Been Through It"
Before You), Resources,
Advice, Ideas,
Facts, Research,
Studies

the strength of their social networks until an emotional event happens." She recommends that we need to build our village with a variety of people in different roles. One terrible day we might need our neighbors or acquaintances to help us in a crisis, when our best friend or spouse is not available. It's a wise investment to foster relationships with our affiliations as well as our closer friends. And better still, we often can develop close friendships with our affiliative buddies over time, such as our classmates or meetup companions or the people with whom we volunteer (but typically, it does take a long time for our bonds to grow.)

Even if we are not in a crisis, a variety of friendships from different networks is generally good for our mental health and our moods—and we won't burn out our best friends or our main squeeze.

For example, we might have a trivia night buddy (affiliative support), another person for long heart-to-heart talks (emotional support), another for exchanging time for childcare (tangible support). And we might seek out a career counselor (knowledge support) or yoga teacher, alongside turning to a couple of colleagues to tap their brains for advice.

Traci Ruble, founder of the highly acclaimed Sidewalk Talk: A Community Listening Project and a relationship therapist in San Francisco, suggests we widen our support system, even with our extended families, turning to those we might not have seen for many years. "When was the last time you called your cousins?" she asks.

Traci Ruble is right. I warmly remember when a long-lost cousin showed up in my life eight years ago when I lived in Yarmouth, Maine. She and her partner had a blast as I played their tour guide, taking them to the best little dives all over Maine for lobster roll feasts. And I've enjoyed sweet reunions with my ex-sister-in-law, who also joined my lobster roll tours of Maine.

Who knows what lies in store for us when we reach out to our long-lost connections or dare to explore our wider communities? With a little resourcefulness, it's amazing how many people we might rediscover. We can check out our fellow alumni from college or go to a high school reunion. And with the help of searches on Facebook or LinkedIn, we can explore who still might be out there—maybe even from way back in the first grade!

Just two or three decades ago, most of us believed we needed only our families—it was enough just to rely on our family, spouses, and close friends for our social support. If we lacked family or the support of a mate, we felt ashamed, as outliers—something was wrong with us, we figured. But in these times, our society is far more mobile, and we move to cities where we must rebuild our support systems from scratch, at the age of twenty as well as seventy. Now it's commonly accepted that we need our communities more than ever before, as our families can only meet some of our needs.

If we take another look at the following Social Support Networks diagram, we might envision how we can build our networks within each of the groups. We can develop new relationships in any one of these networks by *offering* our support, not simply asking for support. It all comes down to getting involved and creating reciprocal ways to help each other.

Building Community by Activating Our Support Networks

We activate support by offering our support, by reaching out, and by helping out. Building community is a two-way street.

EMOTIONAL SUPPORT
Confiding In Each Other
Creating a Safe Space
Being Empathic, Being a Good Listener
Starting Meaningful Conversations
Letting People Feel Free to Be Vulnerable
Acceptance, Respect, Comfort

AFFILIATIVE SUPPORT
Belonging Together
Joining or Creating Groups
Common Interests or Causes
Purposeful Activities
Meaningful Activities
Creative Activities
Passions, Callings
Recreation, Hobbies
Fun Stuff

THE WIDER COMMUNITY
Helplines, Hotlines, Warmlines,
Support Groups,
Twelve-Step Groups,
Counseling, Coaching,
Meetups, Associations,
Clubs, Volunteering,
Serving Causes, Classes,
Study Groups, Travel,
Faith-Based Communities,
Advocacy, Social Action

TANGIBLE SUPPORT
Helping Each Other Out
Offering Hands-On Support
Errands, Shopping
Home Care, Cleaning, Moving
Exchanging Caregiver Support
Help with Transportation
Assisting with Doctor Visits
Financial Aid, Food Aid

KNOWLEDGE SUPPORT
Learning and Sharing with Others
Sharing our Experiences of What We Have Learned
Sharing and Exchanging Resources, Tips, Ideas, Facts, Research, Studies
Professionals, Clinicians

My Activity with My Support Networks (A Sample)

Giving and Receiving Support

**EMOTIONAL
SUPPORT
Confiding In Each Other**

Skype with my brother overseas

Go to my grief support group

Call my friends and family
at least once a week
to check in

**AFFILIATIVE
SUPPORT
Belonging Together**

Trivia Night on Tuesdays

Volunteer for Audobon Society
to help habitats for birds

Volunteer as blogger for
Health Story Website

Show up for campaign
to reelect my
congressman

**THE WIDER
COMMUNITY**

Helplines, Hotlines, Warmlines,
Support Groups,
Twelve-Step Groups,
Counseling, Coaching,
Meetups, Associations,
Clubs, Volunteering,
Serving Causes, Classes,
Study Groups, Travel,
Faith-Based Communities,
Advocacy, Social Action

**TANGIBLE
SUPPORT
Helping Each Other Out**

Help my eighty-five-year-old
neighbor dump her trash

Help my friend get groceries
after his surgery

My sister helps me with
doing bills and taxes and
I help with childcare
on the weekends

**KNOWLEDGE
SUPPORT
Learning and Sharing
with Others**

Do research for the blog I write for

Go to my career counselor
for advice

Call my friend for career
advice, lend an ear for her

See my doctor

89

Popular Ways to Activate Our Support Networks: A Quick List

First of all, it's smart to self-advocate by sending a clear, simple message about what we are seeking and *inviting* people to offer their tips, resources, time, or hands-on help.

Emotional Support Networks

Reach out to people who feel comforting and supportive. It takes courage but keep going. One connection leads to another.

- To our friends and family members.
- To our friends from a long time ago (long-lost friends).
- To our friends far away.
- To members of our extended families (long-lost cousins).
- To a psychotherapist, social worker, chaplain, minister, mentor, coach.
- To a helpline, warmline, or hotline.
- To a support group for the issue that we are coping with.

Tangible Support Networks (Instrumental Support)

To find assistance with our tangible (hands-on) needs:

- Ask about resources or services—go ask your friends, coworkers, human resources staff, family members, classmates, neighbors, other affiliations.
- Call a helpline (www.211.org) or another information/referral line to learn about available services and resources in your area (eldercare, childcare, food pantries, home-care, and more).
- Post on social media about your situation and ask for the help you need (GoFundMe or message your friends). Make your "pitch."
- Go to your local United Way online and check out community services in your area.

- Locate a neighborhood church or other place of worship to ask about community assistance projects. (St. Vincent de Paul programs are available at some Catholic churches, and they can be helpful for assistance in tough times.)
- Call a social worker, volunteer coordinator, or social services staff at a school, university, medical center, government center, or community center to find out referrals to programs for assistance.
- Check in with a reference librarian at your public library to brainstorm on places to contact. (These professionals are typically resourceful and savvy about local areas.)

Knowledge Support Networks (Informational Support)

A few ways to gain knowledge and wisdom and to share our own:

- Of course, the internet and social media. We can learn about most anything by searching online (hopefully true, factual, and well-sourced information).
- Turning to professionals, advisors, clinicians, doctors, lawyers, teachers, therapists, and more.
- Our friends, family members, and colleagues who have been through life experiences ahead of us and are willing to share their wisdom.
- Classes, study groups, research.
- Traveling, exploring, discovering.
- Retreats.
- News media, magazines, blogs.
- Books! (Hello!)

Affiliative Support: Joining (or Starting) Groups in Our Communities
Join and engage in (just to name a few):

- Volunteering.
- Meetups (Meetup.com).
- Taking classes. (Especially if classes meet regularly—cooking classes are social!)
- Travel and touring groups. (Take a tour of a place right in your own community.)
- Book clubs at independent bookstores, meetups, and programs at your local library. (It's free!)
- Groups for dog lovers, cat lovers, horse lovers, bird lovers, and more.
- Being a mentor, coach, or teaching a class on a subject that you are passionate about.
- Campaigning, being an advocate, canvassing, promoting a cause, fundraising.
- Professional association events, conferences, conventions, being on an organization's board.
- Memberships to clubs (sports clubs, games groups, garden clubs, music clubs).
- Memberships to museums (science museums, art museums, historical societies).
- Helping with festivals, concerts, block parties, parades, dog shows, gala events.

A Special Note about Affiliative Support: More often than not, affiliative acquaintances eventually lead to good friendships that provide emotional support as well as tangible and informational support. People who invest in their communities with activities such as volunteering or showing up for meetups are far more likely to develop friendships—but it *does* take time, often a year or more.

Remember when we had to do all that job hunting and interviewing to find that job? Building our social support networks takes the same kind of effort, planning, strategizing, and focus. No, it's not easy, but at least it can be a lot more enjoyable than job hunting! Let's set our intention that building community, as much effort as it entails, will be mostly an enjoyable (if not interesting) and enlightening experience—an adventure.

Meeting people is one thing, but building relationships is another; it takes time to develop trust. In our eagerness to make new friends, remember that people may be breaking out of *their* isolation—just as we are—and may need assurance that we are not going to demand too much of them. The beauty of being a member of a group is that it provides the structure and time we need for building new relationships. In short, our affiliations provide a sense of belonging that helps to hold and mold our relationships together.

Building Friendships and Community: A Brief Introduction

If we feel ready to move ahead with building new friendships and creating our community, I'd like to offer a few start-up questions we could ask ourselves:

- What gets us off the couch, out the door, and into our communities? (And I don't mean stuff we *have* to do like going to our jobs or doing errands.) What are we curious about that makes us want to get off our screens and get out and explore?
- What pulls us out of our shells and beckons us to meet others face-to-face? (A Red Sox game can get even the most introverted Bostonians to look up from their phones and utter a few words.)

- What do we love doing in our free time that involves other people? (Eating! For one thing, it gets folks together, maybe for twenty minutes. Eating together is one of the most social things we can do.)
- We all have different drives and motivators for meeting people. Sometimes we are called to meet others by our sense of purpose or sense of mission. Sometimes we just want to have fun and relax with others (hang out). We can have different friends and groups for various interests. Some friends are ideal for deep, meaningful conversations, and other friends are fun to go out with to movies or meals.
- Do we want to serve others? Do we want to change the world with a common cause? Do we want to learn from others and explore new ideas or new places? Do we want to create new projects with others or collaborate on exciting new ventures? Deep down, we all have passions or, at least, enjoyable pastimes that make us feel good.
- Just for our consideration, I've lined up some ways we might feel called to "get out there" and join groups of people. Here are some popular networks to meet people, and we probably have more than one network we can choose for meeting people:

  - **Serving Others:** Volunteering, Community Service, Serving as a Docent
  - **Learning with Others:** Classes, Study Groups, Exploring, Travel
  - **Creating with Others:** Creative Pursuits, the Arts, Innovations, Inventions
  - **Enterprising with Others:** Starting a Foundation or Part-time Business
  - **Advocacy with Others:** Social Change, Community Action, Public Service

- **Sports/Athletic/Fitness Events with Others:** Teams, Fan Clubs, Golfing, Swimming, Tennis, Volleyball, Fitness Groups, Yoga, Playing Frisbee
- **Keeping the Faith with Others:** Faith-based Communities, Lay Ministry, Spiritual Retreats, Meditation and Mindfulness Groups, Discussion Groups
- **Animals and Nature with Others:** Dog-walking, Bird-watching, Hiking, Kayaking, Wilderness Retreats
- **Socializing with Others for Fun:** Meetups, Socials, Festivals, Trivia Nights, Game Nights, Dinner Parties, Luncheons
- **Introducing the Wide World of Meetups**

Meetups (Meetup.com) offer groups for just about anyone and hundreds of opportunities to build community out in the real world. But it's important to keep in mind that these are all peer-led groups, and we may need to try several different meetups in order to find the right one. (The right host/organizer is key to helping us feel welcome). It takes a sense of adventure and good old-fashioned curiosity to get out there and brave the ever-widening world of meetups.

And if you can't find the meetup that's right for you, you can start your *own* meetup. Meetup.com makes launching your own group a very handy solution. The site will help you gather your people to come.

So, here, just to name a few, is a quick sampling of some social meetups in Boston (I *swear* these are actual names of groups!):

· Knit and Sip Crochet Soirees Meetup
· Happy Geeks of Greater Boston

- Boston Bark Happy Dogs
- Animal Communication Meetup
- Boston Area Pub Trivia
- Fresh Air Walks with Ranger Tim
- Bucket-list Life: F.I.L.L. It Meetup
- Introverts Who Wanna Be Extroverts Meetup
- I Love Regular Conversation Meetup
- Boston Gen X Social Group
- Boston Newcomers Meetup
- "Hey Siri, How Do I Make New Friends in Boston?" Meetup
- F**ck It, I'm Single in Boston 20/30s Social Meetup
- Simply Social Sports League Boston
- A New Chapter 40+
- Culture Vultures for Singles 50+

Joining groups of people can provide us with ample opportunity for making friends, finding mates, as well as building a sense of identity and belonging.

For much, much more about building your community of friendships and fellowships, I have included a toolkit in Part Four of this book.

If We Have No One to Talk To: Helplines, Warmlines, and Hotlines

As we take our first steps out of isolation and into our communities, it's wise to keep in mind that we feel braver and more confident when we have emotional support from at least one safe person who genuinely cares and is rooting for us. Who wouldn't need *lots* of encouragement, warmth, and validation while taking his or her first steps into uncharted territory? Undertaking our mission to build community can be daunting and intimidating, so locating a safe person or safe group is key to help us keep the faith. (I hate to admit it, but I've needed a helpful person to turn to when I've had unpleasant or downright ugly social encounters while trying hard to "get out there" and make friends. People can shun us, snub us, ignore us, or get just plain rude. Yes, it hurts.)

But if we are living through a particularly isolating time, we might not have a single reliable or safe person to talk to. Or we might be isolated by a particular problem that we are hiding, even if we do have friends and family around us. Calling a helpline might be a start for finding the support we need.

Making a phone call to a complete stranger when we feel lost, confused, or lonely is truly an act of courage. It's a leap of faith to call, hoping that someone cares enough to listen. Better still, the person we speak with can guide us to the next step or a resource or referral to a group that could help us. At the very least, we can get a break from the worry and overthinking that unsettle our minds and "get out of our heads" by reaching out to someone. It might even bring us relief and peace of mind.

Though we can locate important resources online to begin our way out of loneliness, it might be more comforting and reassuring for us to talk with someone on the phone—to "think out loud," to vent, to examine our situation, to explore options, to problem-solve.

But, quite frankly, with so many helplines, warmlines, and hotlines out there, it can be confusing to figure out the best number to call. We might end up calling the wrong line or be connected to a not-so helpful person and become discouraged. If we are isolated, it could be disheartening to call someone who simply wants to hurry us off the line and hand us a quick resource or number to call.

As a counselor who has worked on hotlines and helplines and as a lonely person who has called hotlines and helplines (and not found the warmth I needed), I would like to offer a few suggestions.

Generally, there are *huge* differences between helplines, warmlines, and hotlines:

Helplines help us find resources and community services. They are typically designed as "information and referral" lines. Sometimes helplines can provide brief sessions of emotional support and problem-solving, *but not always*. If not, we can certainly ask for numbers to emotional support lines (warmlines) with the worker on the phone. It is useful to specify to the worker that we are seeking emotional support, if that is indeed the primary reason for our call.

- *To quickly find a helpline in your area, go to www.211.org. You will see the phone number to call in your location (often you can just call 2-1-1, but if not, you can find the number on the 211.org website). If you are unsure about how to find what you need, it is quite helpful to speak directly with a 2-1-1 specialist by calling the local number. 2-1-1 lines are associated with United Way (nationwide), and they share much of their database.*

Among other things, helplines can assist with locating:

- Support groups for grief, chronic illnesses, addiction, divorce, unemployment, caregiving, parenting, and other issues
- Counseling and mental health services
- Disability services
- Twelve-step groups
- Housing assistance
- Financial assistance
- Legal assistance
- Eldercare (Alzheimer's and other services)

- ◦ Childcare
- ◦ Food pantries and food-related assistance
- ◦ Heating assistance

Warmlines provide emotional support, but *not* for a crisis. These are helpful lines to call when we feel isolated or lonely or having a particularly rough day. (If we are feeling extremely depressed or suicidal it is better to call a hotline—but *call someone.*) Warmlines are often associated with mental health support such as depression, grief, anxiety, abuse, sexual assault, trauma, addiction, and other difficult issues. Often, a phone call to a local mental health service can supply a number to a warmline.

Hotlines provide crisis support and rapid-response mental health services, such as suicide prevention, domestic violence prevention, addiction or psychiatric crises, and others. Crisis lines can provide counseling to help de-escalate the acute distress or confusion of the crisis and help someone think through his or her actions and decide what to do next.

- *To find a hotline quickly anywhere in the US, text the Crisis Text Line at 741741.*
- *For a suicide hotline contact the National Suicide Prevention Lifeline at 1-800-273-TALK, and they also have an online chat option.*

Finding People Who Understand Us: Support Groups, Therapists, Life Coaches

Meetups Offer Support Groups (Meetup.com)

Meetups can also be a way to meet people who have been through similarly isolating experiences. It helps to know that meetup.com is fast-expanding with new support groups sprouting throughout our communities. We can more readily find a meetup for an issue such as chronic illness or grief or recovery. Meetup groups are created by everyday people (peers rather than professionals) to gather people together for healing from an isolating situation.

For example, if I take a wide-ranging look at the meetups here in the Boston area for isolating issues that are often stigmatized, there are dozens of issues-related groups.

Here is a random sampling of the meetups in Greater Boston that offer peer support for isolating issues:

- Boston OCD Support Group
- Boston Area Social Anxiety Group
- NamaStay Sober Group
- Heart of Recovery Shambala Group
- Christian Recovery Group
- Downtown Boston Divorced or Separated Group
- Adult Grief/Loss Support Group
- Support for Widows 50+
- Boston Highly Sensitive Person's Group
- NAMI Newton-Wellesley Family Caregivers Support Group
- Boston Chronic Pain Support Group
- Women with ADHD Support Group

Other Support Groups for People Dealing with Isolating Situations

Grief and Loss Support: For those of us who feel isolated with our grief and loss, I highly recommend contacting a bereavement coordinator, volunteer coordinator, or a social worker at a local hospice or medical center for a referral to a grief support group. Even if we don't have a loved one in a hospice, the social services staff at a hospice can often provide referrals for anyone in the community who calls for support. Some cities and towns have grief and loss centers, sometimes affiliated with a hospice or a medical center.

Recovery and Twelve-Step Groups: Being a part of a group is vital to our recovery because our healing is founded on breaking through isolation and stigma. One way to find a local support group or twelve-step group is to check out resources through the Substance Abuse and Mental Health Services Administration (SAMHSA) (www.samhsa.gov/find-help/ national-helpline) also known as the Treatment Referral Routing Service. The helpline number is 1-800-662-HELP (4357), and we can quickly locate a group or get help finding other treatment options in our area. The SAMHSA website has a nationwide locator service to link to twelve-step and other recovery groups.

Chronic Illness Support Groups: Most medical centers have social services departments or social workers who can provide lists of local support groups for chronic illnesses as well as for family caregivers. Many medical centers provide a list of local support groups and resource centers on their website. Groups can also be found by searching associations such as the American Cancer Society, American Heart Association, National Multiple Sclerosis Society, Brain Injury Association, Crohn's and Colitis Foundation, and many others. Fortunately, online, we can easily locate the contact information for finding a group.

Mental Health Support Groups: Mental health support groups are increasing as there is a great push nationwide to eradicate stigma.

It is important to keep in mind that support groups can either be peer-driven or facilitated by a trained clinician. Some of us might prefer a more therapy-oriented group and would benefit from the skill of a licensed social worker, rehabilitation counselor, nurse, or other clinician. However, many of us are fine going to a peer-led group (a meetup or twelve-step group) and can also make new friends in a more casual atmosphere.

When inquiring about support groups, be sure to find out if it is professionally facilitated or organized by peers. (I have benefitted from both kinds of support groups. Many years ago, in my turbulent twenties, I went to an Adult Children of Alcoholics twelve-step group as well as a cognitive therapy group and benefitted from both types of support groups.)

For finding support groups for mental illness, here are three of the top national websites for finding support groups.

- Substance Abuse and Mental Health Services Administration (SAMHSA): www.samhsa.gov. Look for the Behavioral Health Treatment Services Locator.
- Anxiety and Depression Association of America: https://adaa.org/ This is a site full of excellent resources for finding support groups.
- National Alliance on Mental Illness (NAMI): www.nami.org

Psychotherapy: In our most vulnerable and transitional times, many of us feel that having a therapist is essential. Before starting therapy, however, it is helpful to find out the therapist's orientation to treatment, his or her specialties and approaches, and his or her background. Some useful approaches for therapy include solution-focused therapy, cognitive-behavioral therapy, person-centered therapy, relational/cultural therapy, to name a few. People with trauma-related issues often benefit from therapists who apply Eye Movement Desensitization and Reprocessing (EMDR). I personally suggest finding a therapist trained in Motivational Interviewing for people who have suffered tremendously from stigma and feeling socially judged—this could include those in recovery from addiction as well as those recovering from abuse and violence. Though Motivational Interviewing is a useful approach for those of us dealing with the isolation of stigma, there are also plenty of excellent therapists who are well trained for helping us break out of our loneliness.

To find a therapist, here are a few useful websites:

- Psychology Today's Therapist Directory: https://www.psychologytoday.com/us/therapists
- Anxiety and Depression Association of America, Therapist Finder: https://members.adaa.org/page/FATMain
- SAMHSA Helpline. The helpline worker will link you to local mental health providers in your area: https://www.samhsa.gov/find-help/national-helpline
- Mental Health Government Website (a website of the US Department of Health and Human Services): www. mentalhealth.gov
- American Psychological Association Psychologist Locator: https://locator.apa.org/

Domestic Violence and Sexual Assault Support Groups: After being able to break free from domestic violence or the experience of sexual assault, we can restore our lives with the help of survivors who understand the violence and abuse we have faced. Many of us who have survived the pain and humiliation of these experiences can support each other as we rebuild our communities and friendships. Support groups can be a foundation for our resilience and empowerment as well as springboards for building community. For a quick way to locate a support group in your area, contact these national hotlines.

- The National Domestic Violence Hotline: www.thehotline.org
- The National Sexual Violence Resource Center: www.nsvrc.org

Life Coaches: Life coaching is not psychotherapy, but it is ideal for helping us think through our life goals, make decisions, and grow our social or career networks. Whether we are working to find more work-life balance or find our calling or sense of purpose or just trying to stay on track with living authentically, coaching is a popular option.

About twelve years ago, to understand my life's purpose and to shore up my courage to follow my passion for writing, I found a life coach who changed my whole outlook on my life. Essentially, she helped me realize my life goals (not just my career goals) by teaching me strategies to build my networks. I worked with her for a year and found the experience highly rewarding and productive.

If I was to sum up how life coaches can best help us, I would emphasize that a good life coach helps us keep on track with reaching our higher goals— those goals that provide a sense of meaning, purpose, and fulfillment.

To find out more on how to choose a life coach, I recommend exploring the International Coach Federation, the gold standard for certifying life coaches.

• https://coachfederation.org.

PART THREE

Brave New Living

Fifteen
Inspirational Profiles

An Introduction to Part Three

In Part Three, I'm thrilled to share profiles of fifteen people who generously offer their insights about how to break through isolation and build community. All contributors have a unique perspective on moving past the forces that isolated them. Some of the profiles are personal stories of recovering from the isolation of illness, grief, addiction, or stigma. Other profiles feature innovative people who have created opportunities in their communities for people to gather and break out of loneliness.

A recurring theme in these stories is how these individuals found a sense of purpose when facing the forces that isolated them. For example, I've profiled Paul Kandarian and his son, Paul, in recovery from opioid addiction, who both took action through theater by performing in an autobiographical play about their isolating experiences. They built community around the same issue—the opioid crisis—that had once isolated them.

Similarly, a young woman with Lyme disease, Allie Cashel, isolated, misunderstood, and silenced by doctors, built her community by creating groups to share stories with others who felt shamed and dismissed about their illnesses. She launched an online support community and wrote a book called *Suffering the Silence* and now has a growing and thriving community of nearly 30,000 followers.

Ironically, the forces that isolate us can be turned into a force for uniting us. The profiles in the next four chapters show us how.

CHAPTER FIVE

Addiction and Grief:

Building Recovery Communities

It's not surprising that families and friends of those addicted to opioids can be just as isolated by the opioid crisis as the users themselves. When I realized that my friend Becky had been hiding her stepchildren's addiction and secretly struggling to cope with her crisis, I forgave her for that terrible time she'd left me stranded in the hospital. Addiction touches all of us with its chaos and has the power to isolate everyone around it. Indeed, anyone living in constant upheaval is isolated in some way—we can't build solid relationships when our lives are relentlessly interrupted by one crisis after another. What does it take for this cycle to end?

Addiction and isolation feed off of each other as a disease of disconnection. Even if we don't personally know anyone touched by addiction, the following stories take us through experiences with people who have been deeply isolated due to the impact of substance abuse. Ana Bess Moyer Bell has many friends who have died from opioid addiction. Paul E. Kandarian is the father of his recovering son, Paul S. Kandarian, and both tell their stories of a painful and chaotic nightmare with the fallout of addiction. Robyn Houston-Bean's son, Nick, died from an overdose. Although these four accounts show us the disastrous grip of this disease, each person finds a way out of isolation and a new lifeline to community support. Each one has a breakthrough and a life-changing revelation along with it. One salient message in all of their stories: Building community is key to healing the opioid crisis.

These four individuals have all turned their isolating experience into a sense of purpose to help others—what once isolated them became a galvanizing force. They now work to end the stigma, social judgment, and loneliness of this disease by their activism and leadership in their communities. And naturally, along common paths through their activism, they have built fulfilling friendships and partnerships.

ANA BESS MOYER BELL: How Theater Saved My Life

Ana Bess Moyer Bell, MA, RDT, is the founder and executive director of Creating Outreach about Addiction Support Together (COAAST), a Rhode Island-based nonprofit devoted to eradicating the opioid epidemic through arts-based educational, therapeutic, and community-driven approaches. She works as a drama therapy consultant for the BETES Organization, creating and implementing theatrical programs for families of children diagnosed with type 1 diabetes. She has worked internationally for the US Embassy in Eastern Ukraine with teenagers who've been misplaced by the Russian occupation. She's interned and worked with addicted, incarcerated, and veteran populations.

Ana Bess knows very well how theater can break through social stigma and judgment. She created COAAST to address the opioid epidemic with actors who bring to life the issues that most people keep hidden and silenced.

The play she wrote, *Four Legs to Stand On*, is a heart-breaking, chaos-in-action story of a family coping with a woman who has lost her way in the grip of opioid addiction.

I saw two plays with COAAST and later interviewed Ana Bess. After losing many friends to overdoses from addiction, she felt called to use her drama therapy background to spark activism through theater. Many of her actors have been affected by the opioid crisis or other forms of addiction. When audience members come to see *Four Legs to Stand On*, they also have a chance to openly discuss with the actors and Ana Bess the realities of addiction in their own communities. Participants find inspiration, hope, and connection, as well as solutions after joining in Ana Bess's events. She has mastered the art of theater in a way that makes us want to make a difference long after we have seen one of her plays—right in our own communities.

The following is her story in her own words.

The Theater I Found, Lost, and Found Again

The only people for me are theater people.

I found theater when I was six years old. I was a precocious kid with a larger-than-life imagination. Being on stage was my way to fill a desire to connect with others, play out my fantasies, and express the deep sensitivity I carried. From an early age, I loved a good story and a heroic female character, and I spent time every day imagining myself as someone else. Theater was not an escape for me, but quite the opposite: It was the way I learned to understand myself and others.

From the beginning of my theater career my mother was my biggest advocate, driving me to and from rehearsals, dropping off dinner late at night during tech week, cheering me on at audition after audition.

She was my champion.

When I was ten years old my mother was diagnosed with breast cancer. Through surgery, chemotherapy, radiation, and being stuck in bed she did not let this stop her championing my dream of becoming a Broadway actress. Somehow, she found a way to get me to every dance class, singing lesson, and audition. That same year I landed my first professional role as Marta in *The Sound of Music*. It was a paid role with a summer stock theater company acting side by side with Broadway actors. The real deal, as my father would say. Although she was fighting for her life, she somehow managed to come to many performances and made sure there was at least one family member or friend at the others.

She was my champion.

When I was thirteen, on the edge of puberty and the heels of high school, my mother died in the living room of our house. It was a hot summer day in June. She died late at night with family and friends around as they cooed and cradled her cold body. We waited until the next morning to call the funeral home. When the men in black suits came to take her body away, they took my pursuit of theater with them. Like her body, my love for theater was limp; the men wrapped it, gently placed it in a large bag, and carried it out through the sliding glass door.

My champion was gone.

My desire to connect with others, to share the deep pain that burned in my chest, and to imagine through play left with her breath. Trauma and grief convinced me that I was alone and that no one could understand. And for the most part, that was true. No one in my graduating eighth-grade class had held their dead mother. Although everyone around me was trying to be supportive, this in turn created a bigger divide. I wanted to scream at them, "Can you just treat me like a normal kid?"

As a teen, I sought out kids like me, kids who were hurt. Those who came from broken homes, violence, death, neglect. Deciding to leave the private preparatory school of my past and moving on to public school made it an easier feat. They became my sanctuary. Unfortunately, when trauma goes unattended, it can often manifest into mental illness and substance abuse. That it did. It was rampant in my sanctuary. Drugs became our church, our salvation. They made us feel normal, made it easier to connect and share our stories, and it helped take the pain away.

I dabbled a little in theater while in high school but found it empty without my mother. I began writing, poetry mostly. I shared it a couple times, at poetry slams, in dark coffee shops late at night, but the terror of returning to a normal life after the rush of the stage became unbearable. The eyes around the room would look at me with pity—or even worse, they'd look away. I felt again that they could not understand my pain and confusion. So, I kept my writing to myself and buried my three-ring binder under my bed.

I didn't find theater again until I was twenty-three. I was living in San Francisco working odd jobs, taking classes at the city college. One day in June, I found my way back. I decided to take a summer intensive course in acting with a well-known teacher, a friend of Sean Penn. I realized quickly that the art of acting really begs us to present our own feelings, experiences, and everything in between. (I can't tell you how ironic it is that we call it "acting," as if it is just a guise.)

In acting class, for the sense memory exercise, you place yourself in a room of your past, examining it as yourself now. On stage you imagine the room, the smells, the sounds; you explore the room, mime opening a book, touching a pillow. The room I chose was our living room, where my mother died. I examined it, the plants by the windowsill, the sun through the glass door, the hospice bed. I repeated this exercise over and over again until I connected with an emotion. I kept repeating the exercise, finding myself numb.

Finally, one sticky July day it happened. The sense memory of the room returned to me. I could hear the sliding glass door; I could smell my mother's body. For lack of a better word, I lost it. I screamed and I cried and I got angry, so angry. And then my acting coach, politely, as if asking me to open the door, requested that I let go of the memory and come back into the present room. When I looked around, I saw the eyes of my peers, some damp, some dry. But no one was afraid, no one was concerned, no one tried to calm me down or dry my eyes. They commended my effort. Each and every person in the room was able to watch me in the depths of my pain, let me scream and cry, and then let me come back to the present moment. No one was scared of my tears, no one tried to divert attention, or even try to understand why I was in such a state. They simply sat and witnessed. That day I realized that they, the theater people, were my people.

I write this now eight years later as a drama therapist, a playwright, and the founder of a successful nonprofit that utilizes theater to address our nation's largest public health crisis. I write this now with tears in my eyes because I had no idea how big an impact that silly acting exercise I did on that hot day in July would have on the outcome of my life.

Theater saved my life.

Theater taught me how to connect again to my emotions in a way that felt safe and contained. Theater people showed me that there are people who could sit with me in my pain and not treat me differently, not even try to understand but could just be with what was. Theater showed me that through story, through characters, through performance you allow people to connect with their memories, dreams, and imagination. Theater taught me that in times of crisis, it really is the only healing place for me.

My Suggestions for Breaking Out of Isolation

1. Admit to yourself out loud or tell a trusted friend or therapist that you're feeling isolated or disconnected.

2. Join an improv or acting class to connect with others and share stories together.

3. Get out and see live theater, music, or dance to inspire you.

4. Write about your isolation in a journal (in the first person or third person) to see your situation as a journey. Explore where your journey might take you. You might see this as hero's journey of facing an adventure (or read the works of Joseph Campbell and others about the hero's journey monomyth).

PAUL E. KANDARIAN: Breaking through the Isolation of Helplessness

Paul E. Kandarian is an actor and a writer living in the Boston-Providence area. He has written countless articles for a variety of publications, including the *Boston Globe, Yankee* magazine, *Rhode Island Monthly, Boston Parent, Seattle's Child,* and many others. Since 2007, he has also devoted his creative instincts to acting by appearing in dozens of plays, independent films, TV commercials, corporate and educational videos, a web series, and more.

Of all the acting he does, none is more important to him than working with the nonprofit COAAST, founded by Ana Bess Moyer Bell. Paul plays the father of an opioid addict in their signature play, *Four Legs to Stand On,* about a family in crisis over a child's addiction. He and his son, Paul, also wrote a play called *Resurfacing,* an autobiographical account of his son's addiction and recovery, produced and sponsored through the Harvard Medical School and the Health Story Collaborative. These works connect us all by letting us know we are not alone in the fight against the disease of addiction. We hurt as a community. And we will heal as a community.

The Isolation of Being a Father of an Addict

I faced an interesting dichotomy as a parent of an addict-child: You know you are not alone and that thousands of other parents are going through the same pain as you. But you *are* alone—agonizingly, crushingly, devastatingly alone because it is *your* child. Your own child. No one knows this story but you. No one is living/dying it but you.

So this dichotomy sums up the isolation: We are not necessarily isolated from a societal point of view, but from within ourselves; yes, we are terribly isolated.

And here's another interesting dichotomy about the stigma and shame of this disease. Again, I understood, intellectually, the social stigma and shame, and I knew I didn't have to take on that societal judgment; however, I brought stigma and shame on myself for *allowing* this to happen, as I believed. We love our kids with all our heart, and as parents we protect them at all costs. We would, without hesitation, take a bullet for our child. But with addiction, there's not a goddam thing we can do, it seems. So, the shame is ours for letting it happen; the stigma is ours for being a shitty parent and letting it happen.

Objectively, of course, I can see how wrongheaded it is for a parent to fall into this downward spiral of guilt, shame, and blame. But somehow, we believe we are at the root of our child's addiction. It's his disease, but it's my fault! It took a long, long time to get over that. In some ways, I never will. It's my scarlet letter, my albatross, my cross to bear. It's getting lighter, but I doubt it'll ever go away. And I accept that. I'll carry the pain the best way I can.

I remember my ex-wife giving me advice as we shared the common goal of helping our son. She said she was going to meetings, Narcotics Anonymous I believe, and suggested I go. I'm a huge believer in the power of twelve-step groups, very much endorsing their mission. So, I went to one.

But, strangely, I never went back.

It was nothing this group did wrong or right. I just didn't feel that it was helping. I went only once. Maybe it was that shame, that "Here I am, the father of an addict" in a room full of mothers and fathers and sisters and brothers of addicts. "Great! How's it going? Do I cry now?" What's the modus operandi for these things? Tears from the get-go? Okay, so you listen, then you cry for them, and you cry for yourself? How could this be helpful? So, I didn't go back.

I did feel isolation from the greater community, but again, that's not the community's fault. It was mine. I was at my wit's end with my son, going day-to-day not knowing if any given day would be his last. I tried turning to others for help by calling his doctor, a state rep I knew, hotlines, a retired narcotics cop, anyone and everyone I could think of. And I got nowhere. In those early days of the opioid crisis, no one could help because everyone was as confused as I was. Correction: No one on Planet Earth was as confused—or alone—as I was.

I called McLean Hospital in the Boston area, one of the best facilities in the country for this sort of thing, and was told that without insurance, it would cost $40,000—every effing month! So that option was out, and I felt more alone than ever, and guilty for not having a spare $40,000 to save my boy's life. The helplessness I felt was staggering—the sense of loss, of uncertainty, of fear and isolation. I knew I wasn't alone in my son's dark days, but I didn't know where to turn or what to do or what to think or how to think or if I could even think at all, as if I was in "the fog of war."

At this same time, in the summer of 2013, my parents were dying, eventually doing so within weeks of each other. I was on both sides of the generational divide—my son and my parents—pounding my soul from both sides like sledgehammers on an anvil. It wasn't their fault; they all had diseases. My parents were suffering the diseases of old age, and my son was trapped in the disease of addiction, which in turn, caused my disease of isolation. It may sound dramatic to say that isolation felt like a disease to me, but with these diseases spiraling around me, I was diseased in the isolation of helplessness to do anything for the people I loved.

It was a long, long, hard, brutal road, but my son and I made it through those years. I may have been the only one to stand by him and finally get him treatment at the VA. He's an army veteran of the war in Afghanistan, seeing and doing horrific things that no human being should ever have to do, which I offer as a reason for his relapse into addiction, not an excuse. But he's the one who found the power inside himself to stick to his treatment. Not me, not his therapists, not the methadone. He did it. He fought the fight, the hardest he'll ever face.

What Pulled Me Out of My Isolation

At the height of my son's addiction, I met Ana Bess Moyer Bell, who was in the incipient stages of founding COAAST, a nonprofit that uses drama therapy as a tool to lift the stigma from addiction. She was writing a play called *Four Legs to Stand On,* about an addicted child and the impact that had on his family. At that time, my own son was in the throes of his hell with his addiction, but I told Ana Bess to keep in touch.

Finally, after my son's start of long-term recovery, Ana Bess and I reconnected, and I was hired to play the father in her productions. I wrote the father's heart-wrenching monologue at the end of it as he begs his child to get help, to find the fight within himself, because, as much as the father wants to fight it for him, no one can fight it except the addict. If there was a breakthrough in my own isolation, this powerful opportunity to share my experience through theater was my turning point. It was freeing to be a father, an actor, and an activist with COAAST, serving their mission to break through the stigma of opioid addiction. Now that my son was moving ahead with his recovery and finally willing to save his own life, I knew this was the right time to join COAAST.

More recently, my son and I have written our own piece, *Resurfacing,* about our combined journey through his addiction. We have produced this play through COAAST and the Health Story Collaborative project at Harvard Medical School. I perform in it, and another actor portrays my son.

By far, performing these plays has been a massive breakthrough from the isolation I had been feeling.

How Activism Is Helping Me Build Community

Acting with COAAST has been an ideal platform to be an activist in fighting the disease of addiction. Theater lets people know they're not alone and proves that when we hurt as a community we can heal as a community.

Our plays are devoted to helping people in the throes of addiction, as well as the loved ones of addicts who may have lost their lives. We do our shows for school groups, medical providers, and the general public. People who show up at our programs are there because they've experienced the individual and collective trauma that addiction brings to a family, to our friends, and to our society. We're preaching to the choir, basically. Each show is followed by a talkback session, twenty-five minutes that could easily go on for twenty-five hours. Virtually everyone has a story to tell about addiction because we have all been touched by it in some way. Some stories are hopeful, and some are tragic.

Being an activist is something I never saw myself doing until later in my life. I think I was a fairly selfish younger guy, loving my life but doing things mostly for me. But when this work appeared at midlife, I took that leap of faith that this was now my life's purpose. Of all the beautiful things I could do in my remaining years, this is what gives me meaning above all else. I never knew helping others build community with theater could feel so good, so real, so necessary. As a participant in the world of recovery from addiction, I've never felt a more powerful sense of belonging because we help others break through the stigma and judgment about addiction.

Fortunately, over the past few years, our society is facing the opioid crisis with more seriousness and awareness. I've witnessed changes in how our society views addicts. In the past decades, addicts appeared to be mostly poor, downtrodden people, people of color, dying from overdoses in the inner city, and no one gave a rat's ass about those people and their families. Now it's the rich white kids dying in the well-heeled suburbs of Boston, New York, LA, across the entire country, so people are taking notice.

But stigma definitely is out there. If I had a hundred people in a room and asked them to raise their hands if they've been impacted by cancer, personally or by relation or friendship, I guarantee that just about every hand would rise. But ask that about addiction, and I guarantee many people would not raise their hand. The stigma is still there. And stigma isolates us, which is why it's incumbent on those of us who've broken free of isolation to show others a way to do the same. Not just one way. *Any* way. The journey is different for every human alive.

Thoughts on Social Media, Isolation, and Addiction

Social media can be as helpful as it can be harmful. Ultimately, it can be a powerful tool to help people in recovery build communities, especially in the early stages of recovery. I do see social media helping the opioid epidemic by giving it a collective voice, to create platforms to speak about it, and show us how to get help.

Yet, on the other hand, honestly, I do think people are more isolated today because of social media. Younger people—their faces, along with their minds, hearts, and souls, are buried in the dazzling glow of a screen that's no more a friend to them than white powder is a friend to the addict—which sounds pretty corny, but I stand by it.

Seriously, social media can be isolating, and studies show that, right? People cut themselves off from other people, so they're isolated and, worse, they're not imprisoned physically against their will. They're willingly isolating themselves, even happily. They think voiceless people on a device are their friends. And sure, many can be. But the person-to-person, face-to-face, heart-to-heart of the human condition via connection is the surest way *not* to be isolated or to start not being isolated.

My Suggestions for Isolating Times

1. Don't let someone's opinion of you stop you from believing in yourself. I think people fear people—the fear of being judged. But if someone is lame enough or weak enough to need to judge you to feel better about him- or herself, then that person is not worth knowing in the first place.

2. Join groups. Join things. Sounds clichéd, but isolation means being alone, right? So, join support groups, book clubs, gyms, library groups, travel groups, cooking groups, whatever interests you.

3. Volunteer. There's nothing that makes us feel a part of something greater—and less isolated—than being there for other people. Helping others helps you in so many good ways.

4. Look up. Seriously. Look up. How many times do you see people looking down, away, anywhere but *at* each other? So, please look up, and look at people. Smile. Say hello. But just look up. Making visual contact with other humans—even if they don't make contact back—makes a connection, that, by its very nature, makes you feel less isolated.

5. Get help if you need it. Depression is a disease that completely isolates the sufferer. (I've had it, I know.) But it's one of the most easily managed illnesses, through talk therapy and, if necessary, pharmacological assistance. Get help. Get help. Get help. It's there.

PAUL S. KANDARIAN: The Safety of Isolation Turns to the Nightmare of Loneliness

When Paul and his father performed an autobiographical play called *Resurfacing* with COAAST, I sat in the audience, engrossed and deeply moved, at times in tears, as were many of us in the room. Later, I was fortunate to meet and interview Paul to learn more about his background and his story of breaking out of isolation for the sake of his recovery. In his own words, in the following essay, he shares how he found a way out.

The Prison of Isolation

Introductions are hard for me. I'd like to share enough about me and my history to get people to trust that I have at least some idea of what someone with an addiction has gone through. Perhaps some readers are hoping that my experience can give them the lifeline that will drag them out of the depths of the hell they find themselves in. Yet, we know that isn't possible with just a single solution. There isn't a book, speaker, doctor, shaman, medicine man, therapist, or Tony Robbins wannabe out there who can give you the one and only secret to overcoming the isolation you find yourself in. And anyone who says he or she can give you that is selling you a load of snake-oil bullshit.

But maybe someone needs to hear my story. Maybe someone knows the hell that I was once in, and maybe it isn't the answer he or she wants. But at least I can offer my humble truth: That there is a life after this hell. That—by reading the words of some other unlucky, doomed jackass like me and knowing that there is even a glimmer of hope of having a day that isn't a complete shitstorm—someone might find the strength to get through another day.

Well, welcome to my life. Even though I screwed up ten-ways-to-Sunday-and-back, I have survived to tell the tale. And, more importantly, I can tell you that you *are not alone*. I cannot stress that enough.

As the captain of my own journey in recovery from opioid addiction, I am the son of another contributing writer in this book—Paul E. Kandarian. I am a native Bay Stater and have lived in Massachusetts my whole life, except for the three years I served in Afghanistan. Like many Americans, my sister (two years older) and I are children of divorce. My father and mother divorced when I was nine, which is about the time I lost the innocence of youth and met the harsh reality of the world—fairy tales are BS. I was an angry, depressed, and confused preteen and teenager. As is true of most adolescents, I had no idea how to process those strong emotions. With a strict, domineering Irish Catholic mother (who had the majority of the joint custody of my sister and me) and an easygoing and naïve, yet caring and loving father (who had us from 4:00–8:30 p.m. Tuesdays and Thursdays and the weekends), I was torn.

My mother used isolation as a form of punishment, which led me to find any form of connection and acceptance I could. At the age of twelve, I found punk rock, which was, and still is, much more than music. Punk rock was a way of life that matched my anger and intensity, while giving me an escape from the hell that filled my mind. I took a few chances to sneak out and head to Boston to catch a show. I met amazing people at punk shows and found a family of people who accepted me. Sadly, Taunton (about forty minutes south of Boston where I grew up) had no punk scene to speak of and the ever-tightening rein of my mother and my own bad choices limited my social circle. Although I had many friends in high school and was well-liked, I still hadn't found the thing I most wanted: true friends and acceptance.

Eventually, after many fights and blown opportunities, I graduated from high school. After years of animosity and fighting for every inch, my relationship with my mother was shot to hell. Even though I've always been very outgoing and loving around people, I had gotten used to isolating as a habit whenever I felt stressed, angry, or hurt. I kept trying to find escapes and a release from my isolation and anger, and I found the quick fix in substances. By this time, I had already been smoking cigarettes for three years, as well as drinking frequently and doing cocaine whenever I could. I hadn't yet touched opiates, but at this time (mid-2007) the OxyContin boom was still in full swing, and my no-opiates streak would not last long.

A girlfriend at the time suggested taking a Percocet 5 mg, which I happily obliged. Although afraid of taking opiates in the past, at this point, I didn't care what happened to me. I had just graduated from high school with no future, no real job, no plans, and no hope. As a quick way to blind myself from seeing the impending blank abyss of my future, I drank or smoked. That first date with opiates was love at first flight. I couldn't get enough, and the funny thing was that it was never enough. After two years, four or five detoxes, an array of drugs, and two weeks spent locked in my bedroom detoxing myself off heroin, Xanax, cocaine, and opiates, I was ready for a change. And I was ready for a solution. That answer came in the form of the US Army Infantry.

Brave young men and women join the army for many noble and not-so-noble reasons. Some go for the education, some for a better future. Some because it's the only thing left to do before becoming resigned to a fate of gangs, drugs, or alcohol. But my reasoning was different. I "knew," at twenty-one, that I would never see the age of twenty-six. One way or another I wasn't long for this world. I "knew" I wasn't going to amount to anything more than just some junkie who squandered whatever talent he had and eventually died with a needle in his arm like everyone figured he would. Unlike those soldiers who join to fix their lives, I joined to end mine. I joined for the sole purpose of filling a body bag so that a deserving and good young man wouldn't have to. I joined to die. Spoiler alert: I didn't.

After basic training, in May 2010, I was shipped to Fort Drum in Upstate New York, the home of the mighty 10th Mountain Light Infantry Division. Although my mission remained to die with some dignity while sacrificing myself for the greater good, I did regain some pride during my service. For the first time in my life since I lost my innocence, I was proud of where I was, what I was doing, and who I was. I met the most amazing men I will ever know, and I will always call them my brothers. We deployed less than a year after I joined up with the 10th Mountain. March 2011, we shipped out. Although I spent a little under a year overseas, I will never forget the nightmare that was Operation Enduring Freedom (OEF) 2011–12, nor will the emotional and physical wounds suffered in Afghanistan ever heal, scar, and fade. I lost six brothers, three very close to me, and twelve of my brothers are now amputees in one way or another.

I flew home in coach, while others flew home in pieces in a box under the plane. I couldn't handle the fact that some loser junkie like me came home while great men like Jefferies, Tobin, and Contreras would never see their families again. Ten months after returning from Afghanistan to Fort Drum, I was given my orders and sent back to Massachusetts.

Even service members who have never seen combat, have never even deployed, and who don't have a mental illness come back to a hard readjustment period. Tack on the PTSD, survivors' guilt, physical injuries, traumatic brain injury, and an underlying addiction issue, and I was destined to fail. There were few resources available during my transition, and the ones that were required tons of legwork to receive. But for a soldier who "knew" he should have made the flight back in a box and not in coach, there was only one option: drugs and isolation.

This began two years of a constant cycle: Wake up, find money, get drugs, get normal (because after a short while of using heroin you no longer get high, so, you just fight off dope sickness and getting back to functioning; i.e., getting normal). The heroin effect wears off, then comes the panic due to lack of money, then find money, pass out, wake up, find money, and so on. This was my life. I worked many jobs, and some were great, but my addiction always ruined any chance of staying at a job for more than a few months. Like many addicts, we hit rock bottom many times, and I was no different. But, just like many other addicts, hitting rock bottom became a normal part of my life. All throughout my prewar and postwar drug use, I isolated and kept the world and everyone in it at bay. Unlike the prewar drug use isolation, the postwar isolation extended even further, and only recently have I been able to make peace with why that happened.

After two years of hardcore self-destructive heroin addiction, I wound up in the Providence Veterans Administration hospital for two weeks. I had two massive abscesses and infections in my arm and left hand. To give you an idea of the extensive damage I brought upon myself during this period of addiction, besides being bedridden in the VA, the doctors and nurses couldn't find any veins to place an IV. So, the choice was made to go through my neck and behind my collarbone. They ended up having to set the IV up on my left side, further down and practically into my heart. They couldn't use the right side because I had damaged the jugular vein in my neck shooting heroin. That's what drug addiction does. Rationally, I know how insane the idea of shooting a substance into a direct line to my heart is; but, I just didn't care at that point.

Lying in a hospital bed, writhing in pain, withdrawal, and anxiety, with an IV hanging from my chest, bandaged from the surgery on the abscess, draining massive amounts of pus, and stuffing the wounds, all I could do was think: I had finally had enough. I also was lucky enough to have a guardian angel working at the Providence VA. As an atheist, I do not believe in the fairy-tale angels from myths and religions, but true humans, who act with immense selflessness and altruism in their hearts, could be angels in their own right. Mine was my substance abuse case manager and nurse, Lynn Deion. She never gave up on me. She pushed me when no one else could stand to be around me. She worked her magic and got me into the VA's methadone program. And I left the hospital with a plan and a goal.

After a few rocky months in the program and telling myself something every day that Lynn had said many times, "Heroin is not an option for you," I finally stopped. And I haven't used in four years, going on five. (It is easier for me not to keep track of how long.)

After quitting heroin, I enrolled into the bachelor's program for psychology at Bridgewater State University. After one year, I transferred to University of Massachusetts in Boston and have since graduated in May 2019. My plans were to study for my Graduate Record Exams (GREs) and eventually enroll in a doctoral program for the fall of 2020.

Yet something was still missing. And even though I had kicked heroin and made positive steps to better my life, I was still isolating. I couldn't bring myself to make friends. My story isn't like others where people isolate because they are shy or incapable of socializing. Mine is different. I am very outgoing, very friendly, and can make friends in any atmosphere, but something in me was holding me back. I couldn't bring myself to make any new friends and had a hard time being able to contact and connect with my brothers from combat. The isolation of being cut off from my brothers and the residual trauma, survivors' guilt, and PTSD did not solve itself when I got clean. I began to realize that this was a whole other battle that needed to be fought. And I chose to fight it with therapy.

Starting therapy wasn't a big change for me because I am an avid believer in talk therapy, but this was different. This was trauma-focused therapy, In Vivo Exposure therapy. We talked and got to know each other, and then we came down to the focused trauma—the trauma that still haunted me. Every session, I had to replay the traumatic event as if I was there, verbally expressing myself through it. Every week, I listened to my recording multiple times, emotionally experiencing the trauma, unlike the times before when I would only intellectually replay it. It sucked. I hated it. But it worked. Along with this, I slowly forced myself to do things that made me uncomfortable (such as riding the busy subway, going to restaurants, and sitting with my back to the door). The retelling of the trauma, the In Vivo therapy, and the analyses with my therapist helped to open a door into my reasons for using again, my self-sabotaging ways, and my isolation.

I was scared. I had to witness and live through the horrible deaths and maiming of multiple friends—my brothers—who I considered my own blood. I had to suffer the helplessness of hearing a dear friend beg you and your brothers, "Kill me, please!" because the pain was unbearable. I had to listen to my brother scream in pain for seven minutes before we could reach him due to the risk of secondary explosives after he was blown up, having one leg ripped from his body, and the other leg's femur snapped under the weight of an adjacent wall. The helplessness of knowing you cannot ease a loved one's pain without having to take his life is something I don't wish on my worst enemies.

And for my brothers who didn't die or suffer amputations, I had to leave them all behind when I left the army and moved hundreds or thousands of miles away from them. When I needed their support the most, I was forced to leave them.

Rushing off and leaving my brothers behind with no time to heal together is the source of my isolation. We didn't have each other for support anymore. We didn't have each other's back anymore. Our bond—our support system and our survival—was torn apart when we left each other to face our uncertain future.

After realizing this and understanding my grief and distress after losing this bond, I was finally able to move forward. I started attending concerts and making friends again and socializing with more meaningful events at school. As an avid woodworker and craftsman, I began to hang out at woodshops and woodworking forums, making more friends. I had to shed the shame and anger I carried with me for years, and it still is a process. I still battle with wanting to shut myself off again and just shielding myself from ever feeling the fear of helplessness—the helplessness of losing people I love—along with the guilt and shame of surviving the loss.

My addiction will always want to make a comeback, and so does the isolation that comes with it. But I have won more battles than I have lost. As cheesy and annoying as it sounds, "If I can do it, anyone can" is a true statement for me.

I've been surprised by how strong people can be—we just don't see it at first, and I certainly didn't see it in myself. For example, I deployed with these two guys (kids, really, since they were only nineteen), and they seemed to be the weakest people I had ever met. They complained and whined about everything, and I didn't believe they would make it through one firefight. But some-thirty-odd firefights later, they were still there, standing and fighting alongside me and the toughest men I had ever known. We never know how truly strong we are until it counts. Though my previous lack of faith stuck in my head, telling me that I "knew" I wouldn't live to see twenty-six, and

I "knew" I'd never amount to anything more than a junkie, and I "knew" I would never be strong enough to quit heroin, and "knew" I should have died in that war zone—well, that was not true after all. I *did* come through it. We all can come through it— and find that we are brave, strong, and resilient. As the saying goes, "You don't know shit until shit happens."

ROBYN HOUSTON-BEAN: How My Grief Became a Gathering Force

Robyn Houston-Bean is the founder of the Sun Will Rise Foundation, a nonprofit organization dedicated to supporting her community for issues related to substance use. The foundation helps with education, prevention, and awareness by sharing Nick Bean's life story with students, parents, and other community members. Tragically, though Robyn's son, Nick, appeared to be succeeding in his recovery, he suddenly died from an accidental overdose. With her foundation, Robyn has turned her grief into facilitating multiple grief support groups for those who have lost loved ones due to substance use. She runs the Sun Will Rise Foundation around her family's business as a partner at Houston Insurance in Braintree, Massachusetts.

Isolated in My Grief over Nick

When my son Nick died suddenly and unexpectedly, at the age of twenty from an accidental overdose, my whole world felt so alien. How did the rest of the world keep spinning when something so tragic had happened to me?

While people went about their days smiling or complaining about the weather, I was curled up on my couch, not knowing how to live without my beloved son. It was as if my heart stopped beating correctly, and I couldn't take a deep breath. I kept reliving that morning of finding him unresponsive and trying to revive him and screaming the guttural cry of a mother losing her child. I went from being a high-functioning go-getter to this shell of a person who couldn't stop crying, who didn't want to do anything, who didn't want to interact with other people. I knew that because of this loss I would never be the same Robyn ever again, and I realized that most of my relationships would never be quite the same either.

I didn't know anyone personally who had lost a child. This was completely new territory. The intense grief and longing for my child were almost too much to bear. I was isolated because I didn't want to face people who had never gone through what I had. Why would anyone want to be around someone who was so sad all the time? Why would I want to go out and listen to other people talk about their happy families? I isolated myself because I was that "poor sad mom" who people looked at and thanked God that they weren't her. Whether real or imagined, I felt judged for having a son die from an overdose and being unable to save him, so I just wanted to be alone. Friends and family don't like seeing you like this, so they try to fix you and cheer you up. Sadly, in those first months, I believed I was unfixable and certainly not in the mood to believe that cheering up was anything that would ever happen to me.

The First Person I Dared to Reach Out To

I reached out to a grief therapist because my family needed help. I knew I was struggling. I have a husband, a daughter, and another son. Nick was my middle child. I knew they were struggling just a badly as I was, but we weren't really helping each other because we were all grieving so differently. I needed to talk about Nick all the time. I needed his things around me that meant the most to him. My husband was closing himself off and getting upset at seeing Nick's items out on our table and didn't want to even hear Nick's name.

The therapist helped with our communication issues and she came up with a great solution: I could put Nick's possessions in a box on the table instead of out in the open, so that my husband didn't have to see them every day. But I could easily open the box and go through it when I felt I needed to. She helped us solve a problem that we couldn't figure out, and she was helpful in other ways. The therapist encouraged me to verbalize my fear and anxiety by allowing me to freely talk about Nick and his death.

My Facebook Friends Reached Out to Me

Many well-meaning friends and family tried to help, and I appreciated all of them. Luckily, a friend reached out with a Facebook introduction to another grieving mom. This mom had also lost her son to overdose just shortly before Nick's death. Although I wasn't feeling like connecting to anyone, I took a leap of faith and we chatted. Our first talk was a turning point out of my isolation.

Carole and I instantly connected. We could discuss anything and everything related to our child's death. Things we could say to each other would probably have other people calling in for mental health evaluations for us. But it felt safe to "go there" with her. To lean on her was a blessing. I would just cry on the phone and she would be on the other side listening, not trying to fix it.

Strangely enough, our children are buried in the same cemetery and that's the first place we met in person. We hugged, we cried, and we bonded. No matter how long it's been since Carole or I have talked, she will always be one of the most special people in the world to me. She opened me up to the possibility of connection in this new world of mine.

Meeting Other Grieving Families

After my friendship developed with Carole, I later became Facebook friends with another grieving mom. She kept posting about this group called Hand Delivered Hope. At that time, they were a nonprofit that did monthly street outreach to those living in active addiction on the street and provided them with a delivery of comfort items, support, and treatment information. After seeing this post appear several times, I asked my sister, Marci, if she would go to one of the deliveries with me. She agreed, and this event was an amazing experience.

Everyone volunteering there was impacted by a substance use disorder in some way. They had children, other family members, or friends in recovery, in active addition, or those who had passed. Everyone at the event understood this disease and they were all so compassionate with me. Even though Nick was never homeless, I had such a great feeling helping those sons and daughters on the streets of Boston. I could not believe how many homeless people there were! Someone loved them and was missing them, and I was glad to help. We started going on the monthly deliveries.

It helped me to feel that I could have a purpose again. It made me realize that helping others helped me. Feeling a bit stronger, I located a grief support group specifically related to substance use death. It is run by an amazing woman named Rhonda Lotti, in Brighton, Massachusetts, which was a bit of a drive. But there I found lots of people who were just like me. Being able to connect and talk openly with people who have gone through similar tragedies was so healing. I looked to Rhonda as a mentor and a friend. She helped me to realize that I could facilitate my own grief support group in my own area. I will be forever grateful to her. At that time, I also connected to a Facebook support group that was dedicated to parents in Massachusetts who had lost a child due to substance use. It is with these parents that I found my voice for advocacy.

Creating Community with Support Groups

Seven months after Nick died, I started my first grief support group for loss from substance use in Braintree, Massachusetts, and called it the Sun Will

Rise. Nick had a recovery notebook that I found shortly after his death and he had written in the front cover, "Please be happy. The sun will rise." I loved his message and used this as my mantra. It was the perfect name for my group. I asked our mayor if we could use the town hall for our support group and he supported us 100 percent.

The first night, eight people joined us. We now have monthly meetings in three different towns and over 160 members. I am so happy that I have made so many connections and have been able to provide support to so many people. It has been encouraging to see the different towns welcoming our group and offering any help we need. The fire and police departments in some of the surrounding towns send out our group information so those who are grieving can find us and know that they aren't alone.

The Sun Will Rise grew to become a nonprofit foundation, and we hope that we can make a difference in someone's life and help them to get out of their isolation after suffering a loss. We provide prevention, education, and awareness for all things related to substance use. We hold a giant fundraiser called BeanStock, a musical festival to celebrate recovery, raise awareness, lessen the stigma, and remember Nick and all those we have lost to substance use disorder.

It's fulfilling for me to observe that my old friends (before Nick died) and my new friends (after Nick died) all mingle together with the live music at our glorious BeanStock festival. Some of these friends only know the new Robyn and will never know the old Robyn, and that's okay. I have a new normal and know I can count on any one of them in my times of need.

My Suggestions for Breaking through Isolation

1. **Help others.** People need you. Maybe it's not in the same way that you felt when you were needed before, but there is a group out there

that could use your help. Even if you feel broken inside, take a chance and go volunteer—anywhere! You will meet new friends and it will give you a sense of accomplishment. When people are working on the same goals, it can be quite a bonding experience.

2. **Go to an in-person support group with people in a similar situation.** I know coming from a support group facilitator, this is kind of a no-brainer. Be brave and take that step and walk into the group. Bring a relative or friend you trust with you for the first time if it seems too hard. Once you see there are others going through the same struggles and see where they are in their life, it can really help. And on the flip side, newer members in the group can look to you to see how far you've come once you've been a member for a while.

3. **Ask for help.** One of our group members came for a while and then started isolating again. I reached out to find out what was going on and after some time, she opened up and said that she was going through serious medical and financial stressors and she just felt sad and alone. She didn't want to burden anyone with her problems because we already had our grief. Well guess what? We pulled together and created a fundraiser for her and raised a good amount of money to help her. She thought no one would come, but when you ask for help, people step up to the plate. One hundred and fifty people showed up to let her know she wasn't alone!

4. **Advocate and self-advocate.** What was the reason you ended up isolated? A death? A medical issue? An accident? How can you change that experience for some other person who might be next? Get involved with people trying to make a change. Passion can

bring people together, and when you make some noise together, it's certainly a bonding experience. When you are all working for the greater good, you can be certain connections will be made.

6. **Believe.** It helps to believe that you are worthy of getting off the couch, and that the world is a lesser place when you are not an active participant. I finally believed and understood that I could do more good putting myself out there than I could by staying away from people. I know Nick is rooting for me every time I "get out there" and bring people together.

CHAPTER SIX

Illness and Caregiving:
Building Support Communities

Finding friends, "getting out there," and building community are hard enough when we are living in survival mode. But add a chronic or debilitating illness to the mix, and we can sink deeper into isolation—and the financial and social costs that come with it. As research on the causes of social isolation have shown us (AARP studies), illness and disability are top reasons for why people are isolated over the age of fifty.

A few years ago, as a single woman approaching my sixties, I was not *quite* sick enough to qualify for disability benefits so I had to keep working full time, even though I could barely keep up. I tried to convince myself that living with chronic colitis (and other autoimmune diseases) was "not *that* bad" and compared my illness to other illnesses, telling myself, "It could be worse," so I pushed myself into job commitments and demanding schedules. I had to keep working long hours to support myself, going against my body's limitations. But at age sixty-one, I ended up in the hospital one day with malabsorption, dehydration, and severe muscle cramps from the bad flares of colitis and other infections that robbed my body of vital nutrients, electrolytes, and other minerals. Quite frankly, the lining of my colon did not properly absorb what I needed for my body to function. After several scary wake-up calls, I realized I had to take my social security retirement benefits early at age sixty-two and cut down on my workload, though this meant I had to make a large financial sacrifice for the sake of my health. My lonely, humbling, and poverty-inducing medical misfortunes have made me far more compassionate about my expectations of myself and others, especially my peers who are living with chronic illnesses. Going to support groups for chronic illness has been vital to building my community.

Many chronic illnesses are invisible, and people don't see what we are struggling with every day. We may look a bit pale, tired, or washed out, but we smile, buck up, and keep going to make ends meet, *and* to keep people from complaining that we are not picking up enough slack. It seems sometimes that others don't know how isolating it is to live with a chronic illness. Healthy people have expectations and standards, especially our bosses and coworkers in the workplace (when we are not able to get disability benefits, although our illnesses have an impact on our productivity), and many of us worry that we might let others down, and worse, might lose our jobs. But even when we are no longer working and in our retirement years, we worry that we are not "pulling our weight" alongside our spouses, family members, and friends who need us. Healthy people sometimes forget that we just cannot always keep up with them.

For many of us, having a chronic illness can make us feel lonely and left out. Indeed, many of us *are* left out. Fear of missing out is a big worry that we often battle—we keep telling ourselves that we *must* stop comparing ourselves to others! Of course, cutting down on our expenses, our workload, and our activity level means that our social lives are affected, and the downward spiral of isolation is a slippery slope to fall into. That said, I have found four wonderful women to profile who know very well how isolating illness can be. Three of these women, ages thirty to fifty-five, have also grappled with their own sense of shame around their illness and believe their shame-based isolation is self-imposed. In each of their stories we can understand how their shame dissipated once they were able to hear other people share their experiences of coping with their illnesses. All women profiled have discovered how having in-depth conversations, storytelling, group support (online as well as offline), and finding their sense of purpose have all helped them break through their isolation.

ANNIE BREWSTER, MD: Breaking Out of Isolation with Our Stories

About Annie Brewster, MD, Founder and Executive Director, Health Story Collaborative; Assistant Professor, Harvard Medical School, Department of Medicine, Massachusetts General Hospital

Annie Brewster is a practicing physician at Massachusetts General Hospital in Boston, an assistant professor at Harvard Medical School, and a patient living with multiple sclerosis since 2001. She founded Health Story Collaborative (HSC) in 2013.

Health Story Collaborative is a 501 (c)(3) organization founded on the belief—supported by research—that storytelling promotes health. Through direct service programming, HSC works to empower patients and their loved ones to build community, to strengthen patient-provider connections, and ultimately, to transform healthcare through storytelling. In addition, HSC programs use storytelling to promote social change by addressing real-world problems, such as the current opioid overdose epidemic.

Annie's work has been published on the WBUR CommonHealth Blog, NPR.org, the *New York Times* Well Blog, *Boston Globe,* and *MS Focus* magazine, among other publications. She has been featured in *Harvard Medicine* magazine and on the cable television program *About Health* with Jeanne Blake. She presented at TEDx Fenway 2014.

How I Met Dr. Brewster

My friend, Barbara Olson, a former social worker at Massachusetts General Hospital, invited me to participate in a storytelling project organized by Dr. Brewster. Barbara interviewed me and recorded my story about how I lived with my chronic illness of lymphocytic colitis, an inflammatory bowel disease. I was asked how my illness affected my job, my social life, my finances, and my energy, and I earnestly shared how isolating it could be to live my illness. My five-minute story was linked to hundreds of other patient stories at the SharingClinic Kiosk at the hospital. Anyone at the hospital, patient or staff, could easily access our stories and learn how we coped—emotionally, spiritually, financially, and socially—with our diseases.

In early 2016, I attended Dr. Brewster's lecture at her opening event for the SharingClinic Kiosk at the hospital and Barbara introduced me after her talk. I was thrilled to meet the person who had created this innovative and comprehensive healing initiative for hundreds of patients.

Inspired by her message, I realized how storytelling breaks through the isolation of illness, and that we needed to allow time for conversation so that our stories could be shared. By listening and holding space for people to tell their stories and learn from one another, we could find our voices, build community, and free ourselves from isolation.

As I learned more about Dr. Brewster's project and her work, I joined her mission by contributing my writing to the Health Story Collaborative. One brave new connection has led to another braver response, so that now I have profiled a whole community of trailblazers who are breaking through forces that isolate patients with chronic illnesses.

I finally had an opportunity to speak with Dr. Brewster in depth about how she faced an isolating time in her own life when she learned she had multiple sclerosis. She shares her story below.

Isolated by Shame

I felt a lot of shame when I was first diagnosed with multiple sclerosis. I created my own isolation with that shame.

I wasn't ready to hear that I had an incurable disease. I'd always had a strong will and had always been able to persist through anything that got in my way—but now, there wasn't anything I could do. My shame was that I couldn't cure this disease even though I was a doctor, a healer. This was a profound identity shift for me. It seemed that accepting this diagnosis was shameful—as if I was giving up. I was mad at myself because I couldn't beat it. So I kept myself in denial.

I didn't want people to see me as a sick person with an incurable disease. I worried that people would define me as sick or would project onto me that I was sick. They might think I was a failure, weak. I didn't want people to feel sorry for me. I lived in silence about it for five years, and only told my family members and closest friends. I was even too ashamed to go to a support group.

Wanting to Learn from the Stories of Patients

I was curious about how some of my patients were coping with illness, especially chronic illnesses like MS. I wanted to learn from them, not only how they had faced their diseases, but how they lived a fulfilling life despite the challenges they faced. How did they keep from allowing their disease to take over their lives? How did they keep up a sense of hope and move forward?

I invited patients to tell me their stories about living with serious and chronic diseases. My ultimate goal was to share these stories with other patients facing similar circumstances in order to minimize isolation for all involved. In doing this work, I noticed my own sense of isolation and shame dissipated. Learning from the stories I heard, I came to believe in the power of storytelling—how patients have control of their own stories. This revelation was my breakthrough out of isolation: We have control of our own stories. We can see our disease as a strength, and there is no need to feel ashamed.

I realized if I was going to heal, I was going to have to share my own story.

Heartened by what I was learning, I founded Health Story Collaborative. All of our programs aim to provide patients, their loved ones, and healthcare providers the opportunities for story sharing for the sake of healing. The SharingClinic at Massachusetts General Hospital is just one of our projects. We also have an audio library of stories online, run live storytelling events called Healing Story Sessions, and use storytelling to promote social change, most recently focused on decreasing stigma and educating the public about the opioid epidemic.

I deeply believe that by telling our stories we not only feel less lonely, but we can learn from one another how to find meaning and purpose from our illness.

My Takeaways for Breaking through Isolation

- See your disease as a strength. We can make our disease our strength. Don't feel ashamed.
- Everyone is broken and vulnerable. That's what makes us complex.
- Opening up is going to connect you more deeply to others.
- It's a long process and it takes a long time learning to live with a disease. There is no right way. Forgive yourself for being in denial. It's okay to be in denial. Embrace your own process.
- There is always a new day—always hope. You can always pick up where you left off and get back up and keep going.

ALLIE CASHEL: Breaking through Silence

Allie Cashel is the author of *Suffering the Silence: Chronic Lyme Disease in an Age of Denial* (North Atlantic Books) and is the cofounder and president of the Suffering the Silence Community (STS), a nonprofit organization dedicated to leveraging the power of art, media, and storytelling to raise awareness around the life experience of people living with chronic illnesses.

While growing up, Allie suffered from chronic Lyme disease for sixteen years, but much of the medical community refused to recognize her symptoms as the result of infectious disease. In her book and speeches, Allie paints a living portrait of what it is like for chronic illness patients around the world when they must struggle for recognition and treatment. For patients of invisible disabilities who have their suffering routinely dismissed by doctors—and even family and friends—the social effects of illness can be as crippling as the disease itself. Allie makes a personal and provocative call to break the stigma and ignorance that currently surrounds misunderstood chronic illnesses. She also offers a message of hope and comfort for patients, encouraging them to share their stories, seek out treatment, and remember that they are not alone. Since publishing her book, she has gone on to start the Suffering the Silence Community, a 501(c)(3) that has engaged an audience of over 30,000 patients in programming and creative initiatives over the past two years.

Since starting work with STS, Allie has been invited to speak at events around the country ranging from private fundraisers to medical schools, bookstores, and support groups. She has appeared on *Good Day NY* (Fox5), *NowThis Live News*, *Lyme Ninja Radio*, *Heritage Radio*, *Love Bites Radio*, and on other global media outlets. She has also presented at a United States Congressional Forum and has facilitated workshops on disability, inclusion, and storytelling with Zeno Mountain Farm.

Harnessing the power of storytelling, she gives voice to individuals and organizations working to create positive change in the world. Allie graduated from Bard College in 2013 with a BA in Written Arts and lives in Burlington, Vermont.

The Isolation of Illness and How I Broke Free

During my senior year in high school, I was the sickest I've ever been with Lyme disease. I suffered neurological dysfunction and other severe symptoms that forced me to miss much of my school year. I had to stay home, often in bed, unable to enjoy what most seniors share in their last year together. My tick-borne disease was dismissed by even the top doctors in the Lyme disease treatment community. They told me that my symptoms were psychological, which meant to me that "it was all in my head" and therefore, something must be wrong with me. I got the message that I shouldn't talk about my disease, and I should silence myself.

When I got back on my feet and went to college, I lied about my health condition with my new friends out of fear of social rejection. People might not believe me or might think I was being too dramatic. I kept my experiences to myself and buried it all. I certainly didn't want to deal with the emotional repercussions of telling people I had Lyme disease.

But all this changed in college when one of my professors encouraged me to write about my illness. I began writing about what I suffered, but soon realized it all was too difficult for me to articulate, to examine, let alone share with others. It seemed more natural to interview other students and learn about their experiences. Somehow, through private conversations, it seemed easier for people to open up and talk about their predicaments with Lyme disease and other chronic conditions, particularly on an emotional level. I found people appreciated my interest in their stories and my willingness to learn from their personal accounts. It was so much easier for me to write about their experiences than to write about my own. Through our honest conversations, I found catharsis and meaning, and learned that we were not alone. For a few years, in our small groups, we shared stories and coping tips, which helped to keep me from the grip of my isolation and silence.

But I had another breakthrough with my best friend from high school, Erica, who had been sick with lupus while I was sick with Lyme disease. Though we had talked about everything else, and though we were very close, we realized we had never talked about our illnesses during high school. We realized that, though we had suffered terribly, we had missed the opportunity to help each other because we had both silenced ourselves. We discovered our experiences with our chronic illnesses were remarkably similar because we had been isolated and silenced by shame, societal messages, stigma, and the clinical assertions of our doctors.

Inspired by our revelations about how our illnesses had isolated us, Erica and I set out to study how chronic diseases affect Americans of all ages. There are 133 million Americans with chronic health conditions, many of whom are suffering in silence. We spotted a need to start a website for telling our stories online because people who were sick at home with limited mobility could share their stories and learn from one another. We named our site Suffering the Silence, and when we launched it, the floodgates seemed to burst open. There was a great hunger out there for people to share their experiences because there were many common causes for silencing ourselves. Our website encouraged me to write my book, which also brought people out of their shells to share their stories for my project.

Online and Offline Connections: The Good, the Bad, and the Lonely

I believe our digital age and social media can contribute to isolation just as much as it can help us break out of isolation. On the downside, I understand how social media isolates us because we see only highlights of ways we live and not the realities—not the authentic, day-to-day ways we get by. We feel isolated seeing our friends fly off to Bali while we sit on the couch in our own darkness. When comparing ourselves to others, it's challenging to share our authentic selves online because we expose ourselves to judgment, stigma, and shame.

But I deeply believe that websites and organizations like Suffering the Silence can empower us to share our authentic selves online. Erica and I, as cofounders, created an open environment by telling our own stories. This has enabled people to post authentic experiences about their own lives—their losses, their mistakes, their successes, their wisdom. When people post on our site, it is amazing how many supportive and loving responses they receive. This is how online sharing helps to build community.

For example, by writing about my Lyme disease experiences, people from five years earlier in my life reached out to me to say they wish they had known what I was going through. All of a sudden, people showed up in my life.

People are amazing when opening up about their vulnerability online. It's so important to be able to write about our most vulnerable experiences. Writing offers a way to separate from our process and look at it from a safe distance. This creates a more objective way to look at things and gives us a chance to see a different version of ourselves. Sometimes, sharing our stories online can feel safer than sharing them in person because the responses of others might feel awkward. Unfortunately, we typically avoid that awkwardness in real life. It's so much more difficult to share our vulnerability and authentic feelings with others in most casual social situations. When we're feeling isolated it can be really challenging to present our authentic selves in most conversations as we rush through the day.

But seeing another person's story online allows us to respond with more empathy and understanding. People can open up more online, and the people who are responding can reflect more and take their time in their response.

That said, we still need face-to-face opportunities to build relationships and deepen our experiences as a community. This is why Suffering the Silence now hosts retreats. We have grown from hosting one retreat per year (three years ago) to now hosting two this year—one in Los Angeles and one in Vermont. We offer four-day retreats with storytelling workshops and guest speakers. At our retreats, it's the small things that allow us to feel connected to each other. We don't have to explain why we need to take a nap or why we need to eat certain foods within very specific diets. We are allowed to take care of ourselves in the ways that work for us without judgment. It's healing for us to hang out and enjoy one another's company, even while talking about living with our diseases. In most other social environments, we would probably have to silence ourselves. But, instead, we've created our own community where we don't suffer in silence anymore.

Allie's Tip for Breaking Out of Isolation

- Locate online communities that share authentic stories about the issues that isolate us. This helps to give us perspective on our situation and reminds us that we are not alone.
- Many online communities we join also host events for meeting people in person. Our face-to-face connections through these events build our sense of community.
- Listen to other people's experiences and show interest by asking them questions about how they faced their situations.

- Find ways to tell or write your own stories about your isolating experiences.

SHARON PERFETTI: The Messy Times of Our Lives

Sharon understands how encouraging casual conversations during the unpredictable times of illness can break us out of isolation. For fifteen years, she has organized and managed nonprofits for families facing cancer in the Baltimore area by creating opportunities for family members and patients to meet and enjoy social activities in community settings as well as medical centers. She now has founded her own consultancy, Paul Partnership. After her own experiences of isolation after her divorce, she discovered a sense of purpose in helping people build community through her work with families in crisis. She shares her story in the following.

An Isolating Time in My Life

When my friend's daughter was hit and killed by a drunk driver as the entire family was leaving an outing at the circus, I found myself almost instantly involved in setting up a foundation to allow the community to build a playground in her honor. That project, Annie's Playground, led me to cofound a nonprofit for kids with cancer.

But one of the most difficult and isolating times of my life was at the end of the Annie's Playground project. I had been entrenched in that project for over two years as a general coordinator, managing every aspect and being sure everything and everyone was ready for the volunteer building project. My phone was constantly ringing, and my emails were always full. This was a strictly volunteer position devoted to honoring a friend's daughter and other children who had died too soon. I had nothing to gain from this but felt it was important to do. Around the time we were nearing the end of the project, which was also our busiest time, my marriage was ending, and my life was about to change in every way possible.

As soon as the playground was built—which happened over three weeks after two years of fundraising and recruiting the build volunteers—my marriage was over, and I needed to rebuild and restart my new life. And as it turned out, all the people who were my "friends" during that two-year playground process weren't anywhere to be found. I was instantly on my own. Probably there were several reasons for this, but mostly people just didn't know how to reach out or how to get involved in another person's "messiness," such as my marriage ending. They had their own issues and just didn't want to be bothered. Ironically, there is a quote painted on a wall in Annie's Playground that reads, "To have a friend, you must be a friend." The playground was nothing but a labor of love for a friend, but at the end of the day that quote apparently did not apply to me. Sadly, I was disillusioned that no one showed up at a time I needed support after two years of volunteering for the friends I loved.

Breaking out of that isolating period just took time. Accepting that it would take time and being patient were really the only answers for me. I threw myself into rebuilding my life, which included cofounding a nonprofit for kids with cancer. Surrounding myself with people who were experiencing much greater challenges than my own took my mind off everything else and gave me a new purpose. That sense of purpose to help others could come in many forms for many people.

As part of my healing from an isolating time, I learned to choose "better" people to have as friends—people who are better at reciprocating, who are generous and show appreciation. However, I have also learned to accept the limitations of others by deciding to move on to build a better life without blame. For me, there is no magic wand, no special group, just moving on with myself and my new outlook.

The Isolation of Illness

After the isolating experiences of my divorce, I recognized how isolated and lonely many people I was serving felt while struggling through their child's cancer. Families and patients dealing with serious illnesses were often misunderstood, dismissed, unappreciated. Up until recently, illnesses generally weren't really discussed openly. There was a sense of shame attached to so many of them and it just wasn't considered good form to discuss one's illness. Now with social media and the opportunity for the general public to guide the conversation, I see that silencing ourselves about our illness is finally changing in our culture. And it's much easier to connect with groups of people online who are going through the same thing. Prior to all that, hospitals and doctors tended to focus solely on the medical part of a situation and didn't really give much thought to the holistic side of things.

As patients, we tend to think, *Why me?* and that you are absolutely the only person going through it and the unfairness of it all. And our family and friends often don't have the tools to know how to respond or ways to help. Probably the biggest obstacle on both sides is learning how to communicate what you need, as well as learning how to offer help in a way that is supportive, meaningful, and genuine. Otherwise, the patient is sitting home wondering why no one is there, while the family and friends are waiting and thinking that she'll reach out to them with what she needs. Sadly, people are missing cues and waiting too long for action to be taken—all out of the best of intentions—because we don't want to intrude on each other's lives.

How We Can Help to Eradicate the Isolation of Illness

There is no simple answer for healing the isolation of illness. These are messy times in our lives when things can change quickly, and people don't know what to say or do. But one place to start is to teach one another and share our knowledge of what helps. Much depends on how common and familiar the illness is. With a common illness such as cancer, there are so many resources available. And we can all take advantage of those resources. Fortunately, so many social groups, support groups, information, mentoring, and workshops are out there. Hopefully, patients and their families aren't too prideful about finding support because plenty of people are out there and they genuinely want to help.

The problem comes with lesser known, less popular, less understood, and rarer medical conditions. In those situations, it's so important for the patients (or parents of the patients) to seek out the people in their lives who are able and available to help and really ask for the help. It's so tough to do. Whether it's pride or just not knowing or feeling too uncomfortable asking, people need reassurance that layman and professionals alike are absolutely willing to help as long as they know what's needed. We as patients and families can help ourselves by speaking openly and describing what we are facing—we can advocate for ourselves. Otherwise, if those professionals or friends haven't walked in our shoes and don't understand our situation, they just don't know what's needed.

But when people do step up to help us, it's so important to show gratitude to those who are trying and who care. People will generally go above and beyond when they know they are being appreciated.

Create Casual, Relaxed, Social Situations for People to Chat

When I was running programs for children and their families coping with cancer, I observed the power of parents connecting in a casual, social way. We developed a program for preschool-age kids to come to a small, weekly, preschool-type "class." The great side effect of that group was that the parents (generally moms) were able to form their own casual support group while there. They shared their challenges and successes of parenting for their child with cancer with others who were going through the same thing. They had felt alone in a world of parents with healthy children, but in this group they were able to be around those who were going through the exact same thing. This is key, and much easier with the power of the internet, so we can find groups of people who are going through what you are. They will understand like no one else.

Create Mentoring Programs to Meet People with Your Illness

I think mentoring initiatives have come a long way recently. More medical centers are witnessing the value of patients learning from one another. I've seen mentoring situations become far more common. Matching patients with those who have already walked in their shoes is such a healing tool and much easier with today's technology.

Four Takeaways for Breaking Out of Isolation

1. **Ask for help!** It's hard, but identify those people in your life who are genuine, and then sit down and have a very real, honest, no-holds-barred conversation. Tell them how you are feeling (scared, anxious, sad, etc.) and let them know that having them as a resource and support would be so important to you. And then spell out exactly how you might need their help. People don't know what they don't know. So if they don't know how you're feeling or what you need, they can't be blamed for that.

2. **Understand that at times they won't be available.** But that doesn't mean they don't want to help at all.

3. **Seek out any and all resources available to you.** This will help diversify and balance out your support system as well as connect you

with people who fully understand specifically what you are going through.

4. **Gratitude, gratitude, gratitude!** Express early and often how much their support means to you.

MARISA RENEE LEE: The Isolation of Uncertainty

Marisa Renee Lee is a cross-sector leader dedicated to engaging the private sector to help solve social challenges. She works with a wide variety of institutions on organizational development, public-private partnership strategies, change management, and stakeholder engagement. She is a graduate of Harvard College and an avid Green Bay Packers fan. She lives in northern Virginia with her husband, Matthew, and the "world's coolest dog," Sadie.

In 2018, Marisa launched a health and wellness platform called Supportal, a website devoted to helping people turn empathy into action by offering guidance on what to say and do for people in distress. "We make it easy for you to respond when someone you care about is faced with a life-changing challenge."

Before launching Supportal, Marisa served as managing director of the My Brother's Keeper Alliance (MBK Alliance), a not-for-profit 501(c)(3) born out of President Obama's call to action to address the barriers to success that boys and young men of color disproportionately face along the life path. She also founded the Pink Agenda, a breast cancer not-for-profit 501(c)(3), in honor of her mother, Lisa. The Pink Agenda is now a national organization of young professionals committed to raising money for breast cancer research and care in partnership with the Breast Cancer Research Foundation.

In 2017, Marisa was honored to be named to the Ebony Power 100 list, among other *Community Crusaders* she admires.

Interviewing Marisa

In my conversations with Marisa, she explained how we become isolated when we are uncertain or confused during the throes of drastic changes in our lives. It's understandable that we don't reach out for help when we don't even know what we need, let alone grasp what is actually happening to us. All too often, we don't ask for support because we cannot find words to explain what is going on. We are hesitant to let people into our lives when we are overwhelmed with a whole new territory of thoughts, feelings, and experiences. It's all too much—we can barely think straight—and we withdraw from people just to be able to breathe.

Marisa shares how this feels and how she found a way out.

Marisa's Story: Isolated by Not Knowing What to Do

When I was twenty-two years old, my mother was ill with multiple sclerosis and had recently been diagnosed with stage 4 breast cancer. I was one of her primary caregivers alongside my dad. None of my peers at my age were caregivers for their parents and had no clue what I was going through. Though I had a wide and supportive circle of friends, I felt isolated.

My isolation increased because I didn't know how to tell my friends what I was facing as my mother's prognosis grew worse. How should I talk about this? Why tell my friends about something so depressing? How could I ask them to help me if I didn't even know what I needed?

My mother's needs came first at that time. When I tried to make plans with my friends, I often had to cancel at the last minute, due either to exhaustion or to my mom's health. I felt guilty and conflicted about how to back out of my social commitments. I regularly bailed on plans with friends and work commitments due to a sudden change in my mother's health situation. In my early twenties, I just didn't have the emotional maturity or language I needed to communicate how difficult things were with my mother or what I needed.

Fortunately, the opportunity arose for me to have a heart-to-heart talk with a friend's mother who was a psychologist. I told her everything about my situation as a caregiver. Our chat was incredibly helpful in shifting my perspective and helping me communicate what I needed from my friend and work communities. My friend's mother suggested that I honestly approach my friends and tell them what was going on with my mother's worsening health. It was time to tell my friends and colleagues that my plans might change day-to-day because of the very fluid situation with my mother, and I needed their understanding that I could not keep my commitments. It became clear to me that communicating openly and realistically about my caregiving role was essential to having healthy friendships and a sense of support around being a caregiver. My friends and colleagues would not be able to have the same expectations of me while I was undergoing this crisis with my mother.

It was an enormous relief to tell my friends the truth about my mother. It struck me how isolated I had been trying to live a "normal" social life while juggling the enormous task of being my mother's primary caregiver. I had worried about not "being there" for my friends, but they reassured me that they had my back after they finally understood the challenges I was struggling with.

In Changeable Times It's Important to Give Updates

When we are dealing with uncertain or chaotic times in our lives around a serious illness, keeping people updated is one way to keep from being isolated. We can simply say, "This is my life right now," and let them know what is going on. We might not know what will happen next or be able to plan very far ahead, but we can encourage people to stand by as events unfold. Also, we might not always need to ask people for help, but it is vital we let people know when our life situation has changed or our roles have changed. We might not be able to keep prior commitments and our regular routines might be interrupted. But by keeping people updated, even when things are uncertain, we can avoid falling into the isolating sense of guilt that we have let people down.

Getting Help Means Getting Specific

My second breakthrough about building my support community came during the last few weeks of my mother's life. I needed a lot of help, but I realized I had to specify my particular needs so people knew what to do. Many friends and roommates had offered to help, but I had to figure out just *how* they could help me. It was up to me to plan ahead as best as I could, and to delegate, breaking down tasks into small steps, so everyone could play a role.

It was essential that I sat down, thought about my needs, and created a strategy for my friends to help. Different people could take different pieces off my plate. I developed assignments for my friends who had offered to help, and thankfully, during my mother's last weeks, I was well supported. Everyone was able to contribute in some way and they were pleased to do so.

When it was time to plan for my mother's funeral, more friends chipped in. One friend researched organ donor programs; another friend bought waterproof makeup for me to wear (so my tears would not smear my makeup); another friend organized a printing party to create materials for the ceremony; and another friend designed the funeral program.

I've learned that most people are more than happy to help when they have a specific role they can play. Conversely, I've observed that people might avoid getting involved if they are not certain how to help us.

Why So Many People Are Lonely

It's so hard to talk about difficult things, even when we do have support. We don't want to have to explain ourselves. It's too much work! It's exhausting and depressing to have to "go there" to tell people about something so serious as our loved one dying or other kinds of bad news. We don't want to depress other people. So we keep it inside us, and it turns into loneliness.

It is a risk to tell people about our personal ordeals, and if we can't find the right people to share our vulnerability with, we become isolated with our stories. Not everyone has empathy or knows how to speak in an empathetic way. Not everyone knows how to listen. It can be really painful when we try to tell the truth about a challenging situation and we don't receive the understanding or the compassion we need.

Another reason I believe we are lonelier is because we don't have the community support of our churches or other religious communities, our neighbors, or our extended families. We simply don't have people around us who are available to listen and sit with us to talk deeply about serious issues.

To do something about this social epidemic of isolation, my friend Jackie Scharnick and I launched a startup called Supportal. Our goal with Supportal is to ensure that when someone is faced with a life-changing challenge, their friends know how to help. We created an environment that gives space to read and share stories and challenges. We pair the stories contributed by our community with products, goods, and services that you can purchase for someone in a similar situation. It makes it easier for people who care, giving them the tools for what to do and say for people in distress. Our online community makes it more common and natural to share one another's challenges and opens up dialogues for ways to say things that might otherwise have been awkward—ways to put empathy into action.

In short, Supportal is a site to help people learn ways to help one another so we don't feel so isolated worrying about saying or doing the wrong thing.

CHAPTER SEVEN

Feeling Different:
Building a Sense of Belonging

The next three profiles explore the isolation of feeling different or marginalized. Many of us have felt that we are outliers or misfits during isolating periods due to situations where we are misunderstood, judged, or dismissed. For example, we might be seen as a threat if we are extremely talented or gifted and outshine our peers. Or if we grew up in child abuse, we might feel defective for not having a loving, supportive family life. Or we might feel left out because we went to school with kids who came from more affluent families. Or if we've been betrayed by people we loved and trusted, we create a shield of protection and don't allow intimacy.

Stigma, betrayal, or abandonment can all gang up on us to make us feel isolated. Even (so-called) successful, well-adjusted adults can feel different from others when we have been betrayed by a trusted friend or family member, especially if deceit, neglect, or abuse is involved. In self-defense, we create a wall of protection or a veneer of friendliness, at least to appear normal, yet keeping others at a "safe" distance.

I wanted to explore how feeling like an outsider can isolate us by interviewing three people who have entirely different backgrounds. Karen lives in Maine, coming from a humble background where her father was unable to work. She speaks about her lonely experience of outshining her peers in speaking contests during high school. Lee grew up as the (apparently) privileged, gracious daughter of a diplomat oversees, but she was sexually abused by her father, and was silenced for two decades. Morna, who is Scottish, tells us how she has created an invisible sheet of "glass" to protect her from being hurt, even though she is quite capable of warm, friendly connections. Just a little bit of distancing from others can hurt us, encounter by encounter, like a thousand tiny cuts, keeping us lonely even though we are highly accomplished adults. It all adds up to a cold sense of separateness—the isolation of holding ourselves back.

But the people in the next three profiles found a way out of that separateness, and I am pleased to share their stories of creating a sense of belonging and finding a way to trust others once again.

KAREN ST. PETER: The Isolation of Outshining Others

Karen is a licensed social worker and an advocate for people with mental illness and intellectual disabilities. She was formerly a licensed addiction counselor and served as a program manager for the Utah Alcoholism Foundation. After sixteen years in Utah, she returned to her native state of Maine to help her mother who suffered with dementia and to care for her sister, who was dying of non-Hodgins lymphoma. Her profound experiences of caregiving and loss with her family inspired her interest in spiritual service and, in 2007, she became an ordained interfaith minister after training with the Chaplaincy Institute of Maine (CHIME). Around her work, she enjoys hiking and exploring and loves the wilderness of the rocky coast of Maine. She lives in the

Portland area with her animal companions, two dogs and a cat. She is highly involved as an activist in preserving habitats for wildlife in her area, and as a single lesbian in her 60s, she volunteers her time for many LGBTQ causes.

My Story of Isolation

I was the youngest of six siblings; the oldest was twenty-one years older than me. I never knew my oldest sibling except from staring at his picture on the wall in my home. He died when he was six years old while riding his tricycle in his own driveway as an oil truck pulled in without seeing him. Though I never met him, his loss affected my family immensely.

Shortly after my brother died, my father suffered a severe stroke that kept him in bed for several years. When he finally did get out of bed, he was paralyzed on his left side, which left him with a limp that reminded everyone of the trauma he had been through. He would be forever haunted by this disability, and since he only had a third-grade education, this further limited his ability to find adequate employment to support the family. Although these events strained our family, the silence about these hardships created even greater obstacles to our well-being and happiness. We did not learn to connect with one another in a way that brings a sense of trust, security, and vitality. We simply learned to survive. And in our deep and perpetual survival mode, I had to adjust to being alone throughout my childhood.

I learned that traumatic events can cause isolation and unresolved hidden feelings that can pop up at any time. I also learned that being different—or standing out in any way—can bring huge isolation into one's own life. Since I was three or four years old, I thought differently and felt differently; I was far more curious about the world than were my family members. I realized I had different views and opinions, a more global perspective than others, and this added to my isolation growing up. I did not act like the other girls and was known as a tomboy. However, I learned to listen and to observe my surroundings so that I could fit in the best way I could. I developed the delicate skill of being able to tune into people's behaviors and feelings and was able to follow along with anyone by adhering to his or her needs and desires while ignoring my own. I always thought that "if only" I could achieve success and be normal, then maybe I would no longer feel this deep pain of isolation. I could be a part of something "bigger" and fit in.

In the eighth grade, I performed in theater productions without the support of any family or friends, who never attended my shows. Later, in high school, I persisted in performing by entering a speaking contest called "Spear Speaking." I really loved this activity and was perfectly happy just performing as an outlet for myself. In preparation for a speaking event, I was required to pick a compelling passage that could be presented in a manner that would draw the attention of an audience. I practiced and polished my speech on my own, so I could privately focus on my technique, repeating my lines until they were perfect.

As the night of the event drew nearer, I eagerly told my family and a few friends that I was doing a featured solo performance for the Spear Speaking event and gave them the date, time, and place for the show.

That night, I won the contest. I was thrilled and excited, but when I looked around the audience, I realized that no one whom I knew was there. Not a single family member and not one friend had come to be a part of my big night. I stood on the stage in the spotlight, receiving applause and a prize for winning first place, but no one from my own life had cared enough to show up.

Later that night, restless after winning this contest, I walked a few blocks in the snow to find the cars of my friends so I could write on their snow-covered windshields that I had won. Even this did not bring a sense of satisfaction after my big win.

But that night taught me a hard lesson about the power of support in one's life. I realized that no matter whether you win or fail, without human support, our lives are diminished. Even though I could rejoice in my success, it simply did not matter without someone else to share it with. And if success didn't matter to anyone else, then why bother to be successful at all?

Having no one to share a great triumph in life was a new sense of isolation for me, and I became bitterly aware that having success in life did not bring the deep connection we all crave. I learned that we all need connection to be able to share our joys as well as our sorrows in life. Otherwise, this world can be a very lonely place.

I've often wondered that if I had been more forceful and insisted people come to my event, would anyone have shown up? If I had stressed more strongly the importance of that night, would I have had a different experience? But why couldn't my loved ones already see how my participation in a speaking contest, or any major event, was worth their time and effort to show up?

A few days after the event, I tried to explain to my family and friends how much my win meant to me. But because they had not been there, their understanding was limited, and I received little encouragement. Later, I reluctantly entered the next regional contest. I told everyone *again* the date, time, and place. *Again* no one showed up. I did win third runner up in the regional district. This was my last entrance into any type of speaking contest. Never again in my life would I venture into performances or contests.

Over the past three decades, I have told this story to many of my therapists and not one of them has acknowledged that this lonely experience of winning without support has had a grave impact on my life-long depression and isolation. They, too, have dismissed the event, as did so many others in my life. Since winning was considered a positive event, they did not take the time to look at the devastation and isolation that occurred with my sudden success. They did not ask questions or even consider that standing alone in winning first place can be as isolating as standing alone after trauma and loss.

This is why I have given up the notion that people can do anything they set their mind to, and that possibilities abound if we simply believe in ourselves. Instead, I believe that positive support and connection with one another is what makes us soar with life's possibilities. Without connection, our efforts are meaningless and empty.

What Called Me Out of My Isolation

Despite my loneliness during my childhood and teen years, I found a true sense of connection when I attended daily Mass at our local church. During holy ceremonies I sensed an attunement to something greater than myself that kept me alive and going forward. That drive for spiritual attunement guided me throughout my life until I was ordained as an interfaith minister through the Chaplaincy Institute of Maine (CHIME). My chaplaincy training and ordination was a true community experience at its core, and I finally found my source of belonging. I was accepted and I "fit in" with all my differences, my traumas, and my joys. Also, after coming out as a lesbian, I finally found a spiritual sense of belonging; previously, I had never fit in with other congregations or seminaries. CHIME brought new life into my being, my soul, and my essence. My spiritual community fostered the depth of understanding that we all need to honor ourselves and one another in our most difficult as well as our most uplifting moments of our lives.

As an interfaith minister, I frequently facilitate celebrations of life and other ceremonies for major passages of our lives. With every ritual and sacred ceremony, those in attendance have opportunities to be part of a community and feel a sense of belonging, acceptance, and wholeness. It is a true honor to create community for people going through times of great loss as well as times of great joy. I like to think of my work as community building in its purest, most spiritual form, and I am deeply grateful every time a group asks me to "hold space" for everyone to come together.

We cannot live in this world alone, even if we are "successful." Maybe that is what some celebrities and other famous people have realized. Winning and being the best at things is a very lonely experience unless we have invested in our community as well as in our accomplishments.

Suggestions for Breaking Out of Isolation
- Take time to feel gratitude for the amazing ways our lives are intertwined with one another. Notice how often we are supported when we least expect it.
- Spend time observing how animals can teach us how to break out of our isolation.
- Take walks with dogs or with friends or family members while walking dogs. The world opens up when dogs are with us.
- Participate in free community events like church dinners or events at local libraries.

LEE THORNTON: The Village It Takes to Heal from Abuse

Lee was born in Italy and raised in Europe as the daughter of a US diplomat. She grew up speaking several languages and lived all over the world. She graduated from George Washington University with a degree in English Literature. Later, as the wife of a CIA officer, she lived in India for six years.

After the birth of her son and her divorce, Lee moved to California to pursue a career as an editor of technical publications for several years. She studied art at the Maryland School of Art and Design and became a successful artist represented by several galleries. She also wrote songs that were featured on nationally syndicated television shows.

A few years ago, Lee wrote a profound account of a difficult childbirth ordeal in 1973 with her first child when she had a near death experience. At the request of the cofounder of the International Association of Near-Death Studies (IANDS), she submitted her work, *Through Heaven's Gate and Back*, an autobiographical account of her NDE and its transformational effects on her life. Her book is warmly endorsed by bestselling authors Carolyn Myss, Anita Moorjani, and P.M.H. Atwater. Lee's involvement with IANDS as an author and speaker has opened many opportunities with communities of people who love exploring soulful and deeply meaningful topics.

Today Lee lives with her husband in a coastal town in Rhode Island, where she provides expressive art therapy sessions for mental health patients at an area hospital. She also volunteers for a local crisis hotline.

My Story

When I was nine years old, living in Finland in 1955, I was sexually abused by my father and this continued off and on to age sixteen. This trauma led to a slow downward spiral into episodes of depression over many years, which deepened, untreated, to a breaking point when I was twenty-seven. My father had told me as a child to keep this a secret, especially from my mother, or there would be dire consequences. It never occurred to me as a child to disobey my father's authoritarian dictate, partly because I was too afraid of the consequences, partly because I was too ashamed and traumatized to tell anyone, and partly because (in those days) people never spoke about such things. There were no resources whatsoever for help, especially in a foreign country as the child of a US diplomat.

Once this secret was planted in me during childhood, the profound shame and guilt associated with it became deeply rooted within me, like a cancer slowly overtaking my body, mind, and spirit. As I grew older and became more aware of the stigma associated with this taboo, this secret became even more deeply buried, like a splinter creating a festering wound that affected every area of my life. As I tried to maintain a facade of normalcy, even happiness, to survive and function in my life, I felt increasingly isolated, separate, and alone, even among close friends because I had to hide this dreadful secret. This made me feel fundamentally different from others—a bad seed, defective, and deficient. In addition to my shame, I was filled with self-doubt and inadequacy, which eventually turned into chronic depression and anxiety.

Surprisingly, a resourceful and resilient part of me was able to function with a mask that hid these inner feelings, even into the beginning of my first marriage at age twenty-three. In the course of the next few years of my marriage while living in India, my "secret" and the effects of abuse began to corrode my psyche and affect my marriage. Nevertheless, I got pregnant and gave birth to a son and, for a time, things got better. However, the effects of my abuse continued to erode our marriage until we began to think of separating. My emotional pain had become so severe that, for the first time in my life, at twenty-seven, I sought therapy with a psychiatrist. My recollection is that therapists were not common in India at that time, and generally in those days, there was a great stigma attached to being in therapy. However, I was so relieved to find help and begin to release the accumulated pain of a lifetime that I was overjoyed to begin the process. I was fortunate that my doctor was so compassionate, understanding, and accepting that I felt safe enough to disclose the details of my abuse. This was a major turning point in my life, a breakthrough that planted a seed of hope and healing that would put me on a forward path of recovery.

This therapy process eventually led to a divorce upon returning to the States, a painful custody battle, and confronting my father, and then my mother, about the abuse, which they denied and invalidated, blaming me for my problems. Shortly after the divorce, per our joint-custody agreement, my ex-husband took my son with him to Europe with the understanding that my son would then return to live with me two years later. I began a career as an editor, but I was back in a state of turmoil over my parents' response and the loss of my son, and I experienced a deep sense of aloneness and isolation. I decided to go to California to make a new beginning because I trusted my employer, who had made a referral for my job transfer.

When I arrived in California, in 1980, I discovered this so-called referral was no longer valid at the company, so I had no job. Thus, I was a stranger in a new land with no contacts, no support, unemployed, divorced without alimony, separated from my son, and battling depression. I had never felt so alone or isolated. Very quickly, I found a therapist as a first contact to resume my treatment for depression. I was fortunate that he was empathetic, like my therapist in India.

I soon found a good job, which gave me hope and security. It also opened a network of friendships. Through my work, I made two close friends who were dealing with their own adversities, opening an opportunity for me to feel safe enough to share the truth of my life. After some time in therapy, my doctor referred me to a support group for women who had been sexually abused. Through this group, I made a couple of friends with whom I got together outside of the group and was able to create close bonds of connection.

One of my friends told me about an organization called Center for Spiritual Living that had helped her heal, and I went to talk to their minister. He was very open and compassionate, and I shared my past with him. He said that though my child abuse history had caused much pain, it had not killed my spirit, which was connected to a greater power. I had only to see it, believe in it, have faith in it, and let it in. He said I could change my life by turning my pain into a way of helping others who had experienced the same things I had. He suggested that I try to rewrite my life, identifying my purpose, what kind of life I wanted to build. I could turn my defeats into victories. This meeting was a huge breakthrough. After this, I joined the Center for Spiritual Living and went to classes there, making new friendships with others undergoing similar adversities, and we formed a community.

During this period, I also forgave my parents. Each of the steps I took were building blocks for a new life, serving as turning points and breakthroughs—the therapy, the support group, making friends at work and, finally, becoming part of a community of like-minded people who were all on their own path of personal and spiritual growth. By 1985, I had gone from being a victim to a survivor, and from being alone and isolated to building friendships and a deeply nourishing community. The final and biggest breakthrough that year was reconnecting with a man I had dated in my youth. After we had spent some time together in California, he asked me to marry him, proposing I move East to live with him. After much thought, I accepted his proposal, which was the beginning of a new chapter in my life. My life continued to progress in ways I could never have imagined, as I continued to seek resources and build social connections. Now, after our marriage of thirty years, my life continues to unfold in miraculous ways.

Breaking Out of the Isolation of Abuse and Trauma

I think many abuse survivors feel isolated and different because we feel such shame, humiliation, and guilt, often blaming ourselves for what happened and carrying a feeling of self-loathing. We are hesitant to reach out and reveal the truth of what happened or else we could be shunned, judged, and subjected to more shame.

Historically, there has been so much stigma attached to abuse that survivors have usually felt the need to hide their experience. We often worry that we may not be believed. Sometimes the perpetrators have threatened us with repercussions that will ruin or even endanger our lives. Thus, many of us carry a burden of fear and secrecy that feeds our sense of aloneness and isolation. Indeed, we have real, sometimes life-threatening forces that prevent us from speaking out on our own behalf, from advocating or seeking resources for healing, or taking risks to join groups or enter relationships. When we do enter relationships, we could be at risk of reenacting and reinforcing the negative feelings and beliefs from our history, leaving us feeling isolated once again if the relationship doesn't work out. Most of us need a therapist, advocate, or social worker who is trained in the dynamics of trauma (PTSD), abuse, and violence in order to recover our confidence for building our relationships and communities.

Also, it is useful for the therapist to have training in Eye Movement Desensitization and Reprocessing (EMDR), a method that helps clients to release emotions associated with abuse and create a new space for the birth of self-love that is so important for healing and becoming functional. Learning self-love is especially empowering for survivors to build healthy relationships. It is important for survivors to interview more than one therapist about their background and pay attention to how we feel with that therapist. If we feel uncomfortable, bad about ourselves, or unsafe, then that is a sign that we should look for another therapist with whom we feel unconditionally supported.

Support groups that deal with abuse are also very helpful for building a sense of safety and support. Abuse can often lead people to numb their pain with alcohol, drugs, food, or other means, and there are support groups for each of these individual problems that can help survivors form close connections in a community of shared experience where they feel understood and supported.

Many of these groups are twelve-step programs with a spiritual base that draw support from a higher power for recovery. I have found this spiritual element (not to be confused with religion) to be very important in self-empowerment and healing. I think therapy and support groups are probably the most important resources in terms of building healthy human connections. Also, in cases of domestic violence, there are shelters, safe houses, and organizations such as local women's centers that provide help, support, and the opportunity to make positive connections with other victims who are trying to free themselves.

How Social Media Affects Us

First, there has been a great acceleration in the speed and pace of our lives, as most of us juggle the basic responsibilities of work, raising families, and trying to be successful in a highly competitive culture. This leaves little time to nurture relationships in a deeper way.

Second, I think the digital age plays a part in isolation because people are more connected to their myriad technological devices than they are to each other as humans, face-to-face. My impression is that our dependence on our devices fosters shallow and quick exchanges focused on the superficial aspects of our lives. I have read that among young adults there has been an increase in depression and loneliness because they are connecting less with one another in the real world. There has been a huge spike in becoming addicted to our devices, which replace human connection, sometimes with violence and fear-inducing videos that increase our sense of separation.

However, on the positive side, I have found that online groups and classes on topics of mutual interest can help to build a community in which like-minded people can share and discuss subjects. These online connections can lead to a deeper level of connection and to get-togethers in the real world.

In these times, we are healthier and less lonely when we have a balanced approach to our offline and online connections.

Lee's Tips for Building Community

1. Look for an organization or group that promotes your values and interests, providing opportunities to form deeper, authentic, and supportive relationships with like-minded people. For example, after all of my close friends had left my area and I felt isolated for a period, I discovered a local weekly women's study group that shared my values and interests in spiritual and personal growth. We discussed books on these subjects, particularly a book called *The Power of Eight: Harnessing the Miraculous Energies of a Small Group to Heal Others, Your Life, and the World* by Lynne McTaggart. With the suggestions from this book, we formed our own groups for healing ourselves, and I made several new friends.

2. There are many Meetup groups (visit Meetup.com) with a huge range of activities and subjects for discussion that afford opportunities to connect with others. I was able to make some warm, personal relationships this way.

3. Spiritual centers, mindfulness retreat centers, and discussion groups provide great opportunities to form more meaningful connections and support.

4. Classes, including exercise classes, can sometimes open up connections. I met one of my closest friends at a YMCA water aerobics class.

5. Volunteer work can sometimes offer opportunities to make friendships, especially if you are working in proximity with other volunteers in an area of mutual interest. I met a very close friend through a volunteer program at a local hospital.

MORNA RUTHERFORD: Through Glass

Morna has been a true, solid friend since my young days as her flatmate (roommate) at the age of twenty-one when I lived in Edinburgh, Scotland, serving as a Community Service Volunteer. We've maintained our close friendship for forty-three years because Morna values friendship as sacredly as I do. She has never forgotten a single birthday or holiday, always sending me cards and little, thoughtful gifts beautifully wrapped, although I have missed many of her special occasions.

Morna began her professional career by training in general nursing with the University of Edinburgh. She later specialized in palliative care and worked extensively with people facing loss, trauma, and death. This experience took her into training in counseling and psychotherapy. She retired from nursing in 1995 and concentrated on building a private practice in psychotherapy, supervision, and training, also working for twenty-one years at the University of Strathclyde, Glasgow. During this time, she trained in Somatic Trauma Therapy, integrating all her experience from nursing and psychotherapy into building a holistic practice. Currently, she is slowly retiring from her practice, "taking space to reflect on life and nature, considering what really matters. My great interest is in how we cocreate space and relationship in an open-minded way where we have the freedom to learn together and discover what is truly important to us. I am open to change."

Morna is probably the least isolated person I know. When I learned what Morna thought about being isolated, I was surprised. I had never known this guarded side of her, as she had always exuded warmth and acceptance. But in this essay, she admits that she holds back parts of herself behind her warmth and caring, and this withholding makes her sad at times because it isolates her from full engagement with others. This withholding is her protection, even if hardly noticeable—a constant source of her self-imposed isolation. She has undergone her share of betrayals and let downs, and has, even as a child, maintained a kind of "glass door" that is open, but still poses as a barrier for her. Morna shares with us how this sheer, sleek, open glass door serves as her protection from people, but at a cost to her soul. It's interesting to think of isolation as a kind of protection, an invisible shield, like glass, as she describes it.

But then, she reminds us, if we have a dog, perhaps there is hope for us guarded humans! She celebrates the joys of what her dog has taught her.

Reflections on Life and Biscuits

I found myself behind an open door. It was a good hiding place (or so I thought). I could see through the glass in the door, looking out at all the other young people interacting with one another. I was twelve years old. I thought I was invisible, and I felt awkward and relieved at the same time. This was my spot.

I was taken aback when a girl with a warm voice noticed me and introduced herself. She was new to the school. I had been there for years. She had spotted me in my spot. She coaxed me out and I felt welcomed to this familiar place for the first time by a stranger. There was a giving and a receiving.

Now, fifty-two years on, I feel the same awkwardness in groups. I wish often that I could find a spot where I could be invisible (but still look out). I doubt that anyone would notice my degree of apprehension. I have now coaxed myself to join in, to be sociable, to laugh, to listen, to engage. But I still feel different—and, yes, alone. I describe this as a state of my own mind, though I have no need to feel lonely. I have been told that I am a valued friend, colleague, wife, sister, aunt, and I have many people to whom I can reach out to offer and ask for support. I am part of many different groups and teams. I am not "isolated," but I do feel lonely a lot of the time.

If you are interested in me, then questions are a fantastic start to a potential connection. I love to answer questions. Apprehension aside, I love that I matter enough to be noticed! And I have learned that I can still decide what I share or not. I spend a lot of time listening to people, so I really do perk up when I am asked a question. (And I know when to stop talking, listen, and ask my own questions.)

When I was twelve, my state of mind was obvious. It could be seen by others. Although I thought I was hidden, I had (interestingly) chosen a place where I was visible behind that glass. I gained a precious friend through my obvious awkwardness. However, I have now become adept (instead) at hiding my state of mind. I imagine my friends would not believe my level of apprehension. This one is up to me. Over time I developed an internal state of wariness. I "watch out" through metaphorical glass.

I have good reason. Firstly, as a young child, I was not socialized. By the time I went to school, it was too late. My awkwardness and sense of difference was embedded. However, psychotherapy and psychotherapy training in my thirties changed me. I became self-aware and open. I felt loved for being myself. I knew at long last what it was like to belong. Wonderful.

Then, in this open, trusting state, I was betrayed by someone I believed was my friend. I felt cut to my core, as if gutted by a knife. I now know that some people are not to be trusted and that it is right to be wary. Oh yes, I am resilient and can support myself, but never again can I imagine opening my heart so completely. I feel really sad about that, yet have not lost hope that I will regain some confidence in my discernment of others and find trust again. But when I shield myself now from attack, I shield myself also from *everything*. I feel at times that the only thing I can count on is that people will let me down. I reflect also on the ways in which I have let other people down.

Am I the only one who feels like this? For me, internal forces keep me isolated (protected?), even though I can go through all the motions of appearing to be "fully functional."

Through my psychotherapy work, I meet many people who are frightened and wary, and they feel certain that people will harm them (again). Together, we deconstruct the past and build trust in their capacity to connect in whatever way is possible. How do you step out of the prison of fear? Before any connection is possible, for some, the first step is a step in (rather than out). Well, this is the pursuit of psychotherapy, but it is not necessarily the only way.

Seems to me that life is amazing in the way that it throws opportunities at us time and time again, to break out of old ways, to take the risk of changing. But, naturally, there is truth in the observation that we will only seek to make a change if the perceived challenge of the change process seems less challenging than the pain we are in. There is much wisdom in systemic theory. And often, the world that we desire to enter feels beyond our reach. Of course, society and culture prescribe formulas for "happiness" (for example: marriage, success at work, ever more achievement).

I remind myself time and time again that the world upon which I gaze—that "other" world on the other side of the glass—is not the world I currently (or may even want to) inhabit. My world is different, and potentially interesting and rewarding in its own way because I am in it and I try not to subscribe to formulas! But how, then, do I make good relationships? I am really not interested in achievement (my own or anyone else's). Is it not interesting to be the orchestrator of your own unique life (before you die)? To break some rules without being ostracized? Yes, there are many cultural imperatives that we live out consciously and unconsciously. Is it not interesting to reflect on and maybe even discuss these? Is that a start to relating with like-minded people?

Before I get to these interesting discussions, I notice others, and I care about people and our planet. I am impressed by how people become the way they are, and I am not too self-absorbed. My genuine interest in others seems to be a quality that is difficult to find these days, and my heart opens a tiny bit when people show interest in me. I guess this is how connections and the potential for a sense of belonging begin for me. In both my personal and professional life, I have gathered much evidence of the value of empathy. Empathy anchored with unconditional acceptance can dissolve both isolation and loneliness. To notice and offer empathy to another, maybe lonely, person is a gift. We reach out offering a bridge over which the other person can walk if they choose. No training is needed. We all have this capacity. However, this gift needs to be received to make our connection in the heart where loneliness is transformed. Reception is a big step for a frightened or wary person and is also a wonderful gift to the giver. Small testing steps are very important, and the result can be a heart-to-heart connection.

The first step is finding "our people." I notice that many people gain real satisfaction from volunteering. They become valued members of a team and, most importantly, they become part of a "we." A wary person will know when he or she is being judged, so our acceptance and nondiscrimination is a vital welcome. No longer are they isolated and hopefully they are valued for who they are rather than what they do. And, of course, they can leave if they do not like it. There is a freedom and a sense of belonging. Perhaps this is true of any like-minded group.

For men, there is a wonderful organization in Scotland, the "Scottish Men's Sheds Association" (https://scottishmsa.org.uk). All over Scotland, men are getting together to build sheds and then work together in them, sharing skills or simply getting together. A real sense of community is formed through being part of a "shed."

Another observation is that there is much to be learned from dogs. Our dog is the sweetest wee soul or so we think! She, in turn, has learned something about being loved. So, she now thinks everyone will love her. She doesn't care how many university degrees or how much money you have. She feels free to welcome and greet everyone she meets, thinking everyone will be her friend or at least have a biscuit for her! But not everyone likes dogs or the enthusiastic greeting she brings. Some people find her approach frightening, presuming attack rather than welcome. Yet she is quite undaunted by rejection. She simply moves on to the next person, knowing that eventually there will be someone good for a biscuit or two!

There is something to be learned here, I think. First, do not take rejection personally because there are other people who will like us. Second, when a stranger approaches, he or she may not be trying to attack us—that person could simply be in need of a biscuit or two.

Our discernment (of who is potentially to be trusted and who may be a threat) is a great resource, and taking a chance on trust can build confidence. But taking a chance involves overcoming fear (you will know what you fear). Mostly, fears are based on our past experiences. It can take a while to realize that we are older and more capable now than then. How do we gain the courage to test out our older, more capable self? This is a critical question. Taking a "baby step" (whatever that is) is a start and having a good supporter of that step— someone to run it by, to think of us in it, to be there for the debriefing process. This process is based on developmental learning and supportive parenting. We see it also in counseling, "buddy systems," and trusted friendships. Only when we take a new considered step with this kind of support and then realize that our world has not collapsed, do we build awareness, realization, and maybe some confidence to take the next wee step.

Dogs also act as connectors of humans. I work on the principle that anyone taking care to walk their dog is a pretty good human and, therefore, worthwhile offering a greeting (in Scotland, this usually starts with a comment on the weather). Who knows where that will lead—maybe somewhere, maybe nowhere, but it doesn't really matter. What matters is that you have noticed someone and that someone has noticed you. This is the foundation of connection. The dog knows how important this is: You meander on, sometimes alone, sometimes together, always exploring, always sniffing. Follow your instincts—it might lead to a biscuit or even a nice cup of tea! The glass dissolves and we step through.

CHAPTER EIGHT

Relocation:

Building Communities in New Places

Landing in a new city or town can be exciting as well as petrifying. We often feel a mix of emotions—thrilled and hopeful and yet the fear of not fitting in hovers over us in our self-critical (and impatient) mind. One of the people profiled in this chapter, Pam Blunt, a psychotherapist who has lived in different states in the US, laments that we typically bring our "baggage" alongside our luggage when we move. It's perfectly normal that our past social experiences—the good, the bad, and the lonely memories—follow us to our new surroundings. However, from my own observations of moving to Boston, I can testify that the joy of meeting people and trying out new ventures can outweigh the baggage of our fears. But here's the catch: It will take at *least* a couple of years for most of us to build our community. It took me *six* long years to build my support system, and I will boldly declare that there are no shortcuts or quick fixes for building a solid community after a relocation. It may take less time for younger people, but it typically takes much longer than we want—a damn long time. This is why we need loads of encouragement, patience, self-compassion, and courage (and why I wrote this book) to keep us from giving up.

We can certainly target our search for building our communities but putting in the time we need to grow our support networks is where many of us, unfortunately, shortchange ourselves. In our digital age, when we can click or swipe our way to instant connections, it just seems miserable that we have to wait a couple of years before we have real friends whom we can truly count on. This is the reason I can understand why people refuse to relocate for brilliant or lucrative opportunities. They don't want to leave behind their hard-won friendships, partnerships, networks, let alone family members, after spending years, if not decades, building those fulfilling bonds. But if we do decide to move for that fresh new start, we need a good, old-fashioned sense of patience and humility to carry with us. It's just going to take time and some tweaking of our expectations for friendships to develop and solidify.

But there are some ways to increase our chances of meeting new friends or potential partners in face-to-face encounters. The following profiles reveal how we can discover and engage with our community with a sense of adventure, keeping an open mind, a "beginner's mind" as a mindfulness approach. Every person profiled—Pam, Ben, Claus, and Jan—has a deep love of learning and exploring. Their curiosity pulls them out of their shells and into the joy of their interest in others. (And even introverts typically like to listen to people.)

I'm convinced that our willingness to listen and learn from others leads to opportunities for building community.

The following profiles could also be useful for people who are not relocating but want to explore their community in their own backyard. If we keep an open mind, we just might be surprised at what's in store on our Sunday afternoon jaunt down the road.

PAMELA BLUNT: Growing Roots When We're Transplanted

Pamela Blunt, LCSW, is a psychotherapist in private practice who lives in Arizona. She works and plays in her studio in Bisbee where she integrates all of the arts into her work (and life) as an intermodal expressive arts therapist. She also offers "Sensory Awareness," a mindfulness approach she has studied and practiced since 1980 (sensoryawareness.org). Splitting her time between Bisbee and the Sonoran Desert outside of Tucson, she lives with her husband and two rescue dogs, who take them for long walks. Myriad birds, trees, cacti, and other wildlife are constant reminders that we share the earth and are never really alone.

We Carry Our "Baggage" as Well as Our Luggage

When I think about the people I've known who have relocated, it's clear that it can be an easier task for those who are younger or who move with a spouse, partner, or friend or move to a place where they already know someone. Many of them were already affiliated with a religious community, a recovery community, or an educational or employment support network so that they could easily connect with like-minded people in their new locale.

But what is it like to relocate to a completely new place when we are in our fifties, sixties, or seventies, perhaps retired, and we don't know anyone? Or perhaps we don't have an interest in traditional kinds of social organizations. Or maybe we move to a much larger community where there are many different groups to pick from, and we feel overwhelmed in finding the "right" fit for us.

It can be very hard. When we move, we don't just bring our luggage, we bring all of our "baggage."

And if we don't have much social interaction, self-critical voices can find fertile ground inside our minds.

These inner criticisms can send us into depression and anxiety. We end up avoiding social experiences because we feel that we are not worthy or don't want to risk rejection. Isolating ourselves is common when we feel vulnerable. The community and friendships we had in our former home base may have been a good antidote to these types of thoughts—but now, without that social support, it is easy to fall into harmful mindsets when we feel exposed and alone in new surroundings.

And what if we moved to a new area because the old one wasn't so supportive? Maybe we were taking care of difficult elders in their last years and it has eroded our energy and self-esteem. Maybe a marriage or partnership ended, a business failed, or we needed to find a more affordable living option now that our income has been reduced by retirement. Maybe some other trauma precipitated our move to a different town for a tragic reason. This can make our situation even more complicated and leave us with very depleted emotional resources. Even if moving to this new place has been something that we always wanted to do, it can still feel lonely to be disoriented in a place where we don't know our way around.

If we find ourselves in this situation, it helps to find a counselor or therapist. Often, we feel ashamed that we are "still dealing" with our old patterns of loneliness and self-sabotage, so we just stay home and dig the hole deeper. I can say as a therapist that this difficult period of adjustment is very common for anyone who has recently relocated—you are in good company!

A good counselor or therapist can help identify and challenge self-critical perceptions when we lack social support and we are hard on ourselves. He or she can highlight our strengths and talents and help us remember what brought us joy in the past. Together we can explore what is available in our new community and come up with the unique steps we need to take to recover our self-confidence. Once we feel more confident, we can begin to reach out and engage in enjoyable social activities.

Quite a few of the clients in my psychotherapy practice have come in for just this kind of help. I can still envision each of their faces right now—lovely, interesting people going through a difficult time. It has been so gratifying to see them reclaim their lives.

Some have found friends and satisfaction in activities that they have always wanted to pursue—joining a community chorus, pursuing photography, and embarking on visual art projects. Initially, the artwork of my clients was a healing way for them to express, release, and reframe what they were going through, but it sometimes grew into a body of work that they were able to share with others. I can think of several who are now showing their work in galleries. However, the self-nourishment, empowerment, and joy that comes from engaging in any creative process is its own reward. The chosen activity might even be solitary, but it can reawaken your self-confidence and passion for living. From there, building community is much easier. More often than not, our interests will lead us to other people who share them.

If you are shy, you may always be shy. You don't have to wait until you overcome your shyness to begin to reach out socially. Start by intentionally choosing events or activities that are not overwhelming. For example, some social activities don't require much conversation or they are focused on very specific activities that make conversation easier.

Everywhere you go, there will be people just as shy as you are. In fact, those really confident people you see may have also felt alone and scared not so long ago when they first came to town. They may have experienced some trauma or loss themselves. I know this is true because this happened to me. I have had to come to terms with my own traumatic experiences. I have relocated to vastly different states in my own lifetime (Maine, Florida, and Arizona, starting out as a Virginia native). I remember how shy and uncertain I was about reaching out to others. It could happen to me again when life gets hard.

Our support networks can change throughout our lives, even if we are "well-connected." Hopefully, we can hold onto a few friends throughout the years, across the miles, and despite the isolating times in our lives. And we can create new connections wherever we are.

And it doesn't have to cost much. These days photography and video production are doable with a smartphone. Community choruses don't cost anything to join. Hiking clubs, birding groups, and fiber arts collectives are often free or cost very little. Astronomy stores offer regular stargazing events. Lifelong learning programs offer classes at a discounted tuition.

If we are unable to drive due to physical limitations, many cities offer public transportation at a reduced rate. Some towns even offer door-to-door options for those who need it.

More Tips for Building Community Networks

- Look deeply at your interests, even if you feel down right now. What is available in your new locale? Go into or call stores with related products or content to ask what kinds of groups they know about. Search online. Many groups send out regular newsletters about their events in your area.
- Get help if you are feeling hopeless about starting your new life and you find yourself self-sabotaging. It is very hard to overcome self-criticism on your own and you don't need to do this alone.
- Remember that other people are feeling lonely, too, and they might very well welcome it when you reach out.
- Remind yourself that your loneliness does not indicate there is anything wrong with you. Our society has changed a great deal. This issue is bigger than any of us and we share the fallout with so many other people.

- There are many volunteer opportunities in all kinds of organizations: The Audubon Society for bird lovers, wildlife groups that need members to do fieldwork, reading to and tutoring children in the schools, historical societies, arts collectives, animal rescue shelters, political groups, and more. Commitments can be small or ongoing. Again: Search online for your interests to find out about local organizations.
- Newcomers groups and Meetup.com can offer social opportunities for relocated people.
- Stay in touch with old friends who celebrate who you are. Even if they are now far away, their support is crucial. Open up to them honestly. We are not meant to be "rugged individualists." Introverted or extroverted, we are social creatures.
- For some people, part-time, rewarding work has ended up connecting them with new friends and local groups.

CLAUS ADAM JARLOV: Creating Sanctuaries of Belonging

How I Met Claus

As an adventurous young hippie in the early 1970s, I traveled with my knapsack and flute all over Europe and lived in youth hostels, on friend's sofas, and on benches in train stations. A high school friend of mine introduced me to her friends in Copenhagen, Denmark, and I met Claus Adam Jarlov at a school dance. We both played the flute and discovered we loved Baroque music, though he performed far better than I.

Somehow, over the decades, we have stayed in touch, mostly as pen pals, and we chat on the phone on occasion. He cheers me up with his hope for humanity as he witnesses through his company how cross-cultural communication helps build a sense of community, even these days in today's (not so civil) climate. He believes that in very small ways we can build our own sanctuaries of trust by "being interested in learning about the other side," as he puts it.

Being interested in what the "other side" has to say may seem simple and obvious, but putting this into practice every day with people from diverse backgrounds is truly an art. Claus has developed and expressed this fine art through his career and his company, so I asked him to weigh in with his thoughts about isolation and loneliness.

About Claus Adam Jarlov

Claus is the CEO and founder of GlobalDenmark in Copenhagen, a company that provides training and consulting in cross-cultural communication. His company includes eleven consultants who work primarily for Danish companies and universities. Claus has been involved in projects in Ethiopia, Spain, Morocco, the US, Russia, and the Nordic countries, focusing on communicating across national, professional, and personal borders. Claus and his team also provide courses on academic communication for PhD candidates from all over the world doing their research program in Denmark. He has an MA in English and Psychology from the University of Copenhagen. Prior to launching GlobalDenmark, he was a language and negotiation consultant for the Danish Ministry of Foreign Affairs Language Centre.

Claus is married to a musicologist and musician who plays the harpsichord. He still plays the flute and specializes in Baroque music. He and his wife, Hannah, are both eighteenth-century music enthusiasts, and they met while performing at a concert together: "A flute sonata brought us together." They have two children and three grandchildren. In 1984, Claus and Hannah started their first company together, and then developed five more businesses, ranging from cross-cultural communication to making classical music known to a wider audience.

Claus believes that love, music, and business are the building blocks of his marriage and family as well as his professional life.

In his own view of loneliness in Denmark, his stance is that Danes are generally outgoing and sociable, and yet loneliness is widespread (though it is hidden.) Claus also knows how isolation feels. He shares his own story in the following.

When I Felt Isolated

I was always seen as the jovial and extroverted one in my family and loved lively conversations and people. My younger brother was in many regards perceived as my opposite, quite introverted. Whether our surroundings defined us or it was in fact part of our personalities, we didn't get along terribly well throughout our childhood. We were not on the same wavelength; I was loud and potentially superficial, and he was quiet and more profound. Or so it seemed. Stereotyping children is tricky. My mother took a protective stance toward our relationship, trying hard to avoid conflicts and quarrels between us. For decades, my brother and I kept a distance because our personalities were so different. Our wives and children kept us together.

But everything changed when my mother died in 2017. My father had died seventeen years earlier, and my mother was able to create a new life for herself after forty-eight years of marriage. She was a strong fighter and able to establish true and lasting relationships—real friendships and the natural center of a large family. I was attached to both my parents, but the death of my mother left me feeling deeply shaken and lost; now I had no parents. Without my mother, there was no bridge between my brother and me. I withdrew from him, assuming it would be useless trying to talk to him about my feelings. Even though I had a loving wife and family to support me, I was utterly frozen at trying to connect with my brother. This wall created a sense of isolation and helplessness inside me that I had hardly ever felt before.

And then, a few months after my mother's funeral, out of the blue, I realized that my brother was reaching out to *me*. He opened up and shared his emotions, genuinely trying to connect with me. Somehow, the loss of our mother allowed a whole new opportunity for my brother and me to connect in ways we had never done before. I was now in a receptive mode and was able to listen to him and let him express himself in ways I had never known in my life.

Since my mother's death, my brother and I have been closer than ever before. I have learned from this experience that we can be isolated when our roles suddenly change, and we don't know how to act or what to do with our new identity. I had been the outgoing, confident brother and suddenly I was lost. But this created the space for my sensitive, quieter brother to speak up. The grief that had isolated me at first actually became the opportunity for us to connect. My mother's death gave my brother and me space to eventually connect. My mother succeeded posthumously in bringing us together. I am deeply grateful to her for enabling us to break through decades of disconnection.

Sanctuaries Help Us Make Connections

When my kids went to high school, I volunteered on the board of their school and served as a mentor for teens. I was amazed how teens from well-to-do families would experience loneliness at home. They told me no one listened to them and that their parents were working too much and too distracted. (And this was in the in the 1990s before smartphones and social media!) It struck me that just by providing a quiet space to listen one-on-one could be profoundly healing. Working with the teachers and hanging out with these kids proved to me that people need sanctuaries (safe spaces) for casual and private conversations without judgment or expectations. I learned the value of having a regular, consistent time and place for people to come and talk—building interest in the "other side."

Creating small, casual groups, like sanctuaries, is one way to help people break out of isolation and build community. I've applied this concept to my intercultural initiatives at my company, GlobalDenmark. Through my work as a coach for business executives, politicians, and researchers, I have discovered that even people who have successful careers and seem to have everything under control can feel isolated and lonely. They may have hundreds of admirers and colleagues, and yet no one to go to when there is "that stone in the shoe." One of my most powerful tools as a coach is to be totally present with my client in a safe, confidential space. Mutual presence is a prerequisite for openness and trust—the way out of isolation.

Over the years, I have facilitated workshops in Denmark for PhD candidates from all over the world. We teach scientific communication across borders. International students can be quite isolated in Denmark. Some want to isolate themselves and others simply end up being very lonely. Our workshops allow time for the students to get to know one another over a meal. They can talk to the workshop facilitators about how they are coping with intercultural issues and their personal difficulties while trying to adapt to a Danish culture that is so different from theirs. I've frequently observed that students feel freer to express themselves while speaking English than in their native Chinese, Danish, or Italian—a shared foreign language opens the door to candidness and trust! Speaking a foreign language breaks them out of their shells. Our mother tongue can actually be an inhibitor. I've learned that people are more likely to try out new social interactions and behaviors when they communicate in a language that is different from their mother tongue. Fortunately, in small, private groups we feel free enough to build community by trying out new perspectives and approaches. A foreign language can be a catalyst for new ideas and perspectives and for building new relationships.

Thoughts about Screen Time in Denmark

In Denmark, I've observed younger adults and teens spend more time onscreen. I see a difference from ten years ago. I recently saw a woman almost get run over by a car while crossing the street because her head was down reading her screen. I think we are now too absorbed in our screens, which means we might be too *self*-absorbed. Maybe I'm just getting old; maybe young people can create relationships while being absorbed in a smartphone. Of course, it's undeniably harder to make eye contact and spark a casual conversation while engaged in an update on the phone. Social media uses words like "conversation" and "friends," but I just wonder if this is real conversation and making real friends. Conversations, as I have learned to appreciate them over the past six decades, have now become more short-lived when they happen spontaneously. This is very unfortunate. Real conversations and real friendships are founded on our interest in the other side. This is how magic happens in our lives!

And we need that magic now.

BEN RIGGS: Building Community through the Love of Learning

Out of the blue, I received an email from Ben inviting me to speak at a group called the Circle of Scholars in Newport, Rhode Island. He had heard from his wife about a course I taught on how to comfort others and quickly organized a large forum for a discussion. Not only did he offer his graciousness and generosity as a host when I arrived to speak, but he shared with me his passion for lifelong learning initiatives that offered seniors ways to build community.

He gave me a tour of the historic Edward King House where Circle of Scholars holds its programs—not your average senior center, but full of rooms for studying, teaching, creating, storytelling, and socializing.

Ben fiercely believes that the power of our curiosity and our love of learning give us the courage to break out of isolation. People come from all walks of life to the programs to learn as well as to teach, and his warmth and interest in others sparks conversations with newcomers and anyone venturing out to explore new ideas.

He organizes and encourages seniors—many of whom have never taught a course in their entire lives—to teach what they love. He frequently meets people who are hungry to teach about a topic that captivates them, to share their wisdom and their skills with others, long after their retirement. Fostering these exchanges of teaching, mentoring, and learning, Ben witnesses how these meaningful encounters build community for seniors who may otherwise be isolated at home.

In 2000, Ben and his wife, Lee, moved to Newport, Rhode Island, to enjoy the local sailing community. He is actively engaged in sail training programs at the naval station and is enthusiastically involved in his community promoting education for seniors. He is a former president of the Salve Regina University Circle of Scholars and most recently served as the president of the Newport Circle of Scholars at the Edward King House. He is also the founder and group leader of the Rhode Island Chapter of the International Association for Near-Death Studies (IANDS).

He continues to work part time as a managing director of Resource Management Company, LLC, a small investment banking business operating out of Newport, Rhode Island, and Palm City, Florida. He previously spent more than fifteen years managing several manufacturing companies and completed and integrated numerous acquisitions as COO/CEO.

Ben earned his BA from Boston University in 1968. After college, Ben served as a US Navy pilot, flying the A-7 Corsair II light attack aircraft aboard the USS Independence. For fourteen years he served in the Air Systems Program of the Naval Reserve as Aeronautical Engineering Duty Officer and was later Commanding Officer of his unit. He is now retired as a Captain.

What Keeps Me from Feeling Isolated

My responsibilities and my sense of service to others have kept me from feeling isolated for most of my life. First of all, I was busy facing the challenges of working my way through college full time while being responsible for my recently divorced mother (who by then had started battling a long bout with cancer) and two younger brothers. There was little time for worrying about myself.

As a Navy pilot flying off an aircraft carrier, I also had to focus on staying alive. Yet, when my mother finally died, I suffered from depression and started losing concentration. After a very close call landing my plane on the ship one night, the Navy took me out of action for six weeks while I had therapy. It seemed to work, and I went back to flying without any more problems.

Finally, another reason I didn't fall into isolation is that I had a demanding yet socially interactive job with a heavy travel schedule while I raised my children.

But on a deeper level, especially as I've become older, I've found it rewarding to share knowledge with others as well as to keep learning from others. Through my involvement in the Newport community, I've taught sailing skills to naval personnel and their families. Not only have I enjoyed the relationships with other instructors and the experience of teaching hundreds of diverse people how to sail over the years, but I've became a better teacher and sailor in the process. I've become close friends with my fellow instructors, and we've often traveled together to the Caribbean in the winter to sail.

Sailing is my personal passion; yet, generally, I've discovered that lifelong learning programs and community education centers provide many ways to keep our minds healthy and engaged. In short, a love of learning keeps us from becoming isolated. Courses invite us to join as a group with similar interests, and we can get to know one another more deeply through the discussions that take place during and, especially, after the class. Friendships naturally grow from heartfelt and meaningful conversations, which lead us to bond through our common values. The more we share our values, we realize that our classmates have many of the same fears and desires as we do—and this fosters trust and closeness.

The learning process during our later years is different in that we are choosing classes based on what interests us instead of having to meet requirements for a degree or a career move. Also, because we have stopped caring about our public images, we are not afraid to ask questions and even to disagree with the teacher. Many of us become more curious and open-minded as we mature.

Still, at any age, interactive learning stimulates the mind more than, say, passive reading does, and it gives us a sense of purpose and connection, which frees us from isolation. Most of us desire more meaningful conversation—indeed, exploring the meaning of life together is a wonderful way to build lifelong friendships!

My Suggestions for Breaking Out of Isolation

- Start by telling the person in the mirror each day that you are empowered with love and kindness.

- Try to see the love and kindness in others, while you surround yourself with like-minded people.

- Follow your own instincts about what is best for you, while striving to leave this Earth a little bit better than you found it.

- Don't put off doing the things you are still able to do. Most in life can be achieved just by showing up.

- Live fearlessly, knowing that when your body finally dies, you will go on without it, returning with joy to the place from which you first came.

JAN MAIER: A World of Friendships

I first met Jan on a bright June afternoon in 1996 at a women's spiritual retreat in a monastery in Rochester, Minnesota. A musician and singer, she led a group of fifty women in a sacred song to honor our grief over our life's losses. Jan drew us into a sense of belonging, trusting that through our singing and harmonies we could support one another and no longer needed to be alone in our pain. This powerful event opened my heart and mind to the ways music could move us to break out of our isolation and separateness.

To my great surprise, almost twenty years later in 2015, I ran into Jan at a Fourth of July party on a friend's porch in Boston. We sat on lawn chairs and ate watermelon while we caught up on our lives. She is now a consultant who trains caregivers to use music with people who have dementia.

What impresses me about Jan is her zest for life, love of learning, traveling, and interest in others. She exudes warmth, curiosity, and generosity, and enjoys a wide network of friends and partnerships around the world. With a gift for putting people at ease, she listens deeply to people when they talk with her, and everywhere she goes, she is a magnet for welcoming and lively conversation. She seems to belong anywhere and everywhere—as if the world was her oyster.

Jan and I are both single and childless women in our sixties. I have found Jan to be a brilliant role model for me as I look into aging gracefully with a strong circle of friends and community partnerships. Jan has inspired me to trust that my sense of security is ultimately founded on my solid safety net of community support. I invited Jan to share her insights on building community.

Lifelong Curiosity Creates Lifelong Community

My life resembles a colorful patchwork quilt rather than one with a single theme. I have lived many places and had several concurrent career paths. For income and the rewards of helping others, I chose community health and psychiatric nursing, health education, and health policy research. For my passion in music, I pursued a wide variety of work in teaching, conducting, performing, recording, composing, and singing. Since 2000, I have worked part-time so I would have the energy and time left for my music endeavors, though they produced little income. I moved nearly twenty times in as many years in order to spend as little as possible on housing so I could travel. I managed to do quite a bit of world travel, always on half a shoe-string—yet filled with adventure!

I have yet to find a life-long partner but had several long-term relationships. I never had children or owned a home, but I would have enjoyed both. I've had a wonderfully supportive family who were always very close in heart, but I've lost my younger brother and both parents. My immediate family has now dwindled to my very dear older sister and myself.

Following my passions converted me from an introvert to an outgoing person. I have learned to reach out to people, take risks, establish and maintain friendships and, as a result, have built several long-lasting communities spanning many miles and decades. If one thing has led me to more friendships than any other, it is my passion for music. I thrive in sharing music and creating harmony with others (literally and figuratively), meeting new people from other cultures, making new friends, laughter, and traveling to new places.

In my recent retirement, I'm making road trips to visit friends and relatives, traveling as far as the budget allows, and developing networks across the country and the world for leading my workshops for caregivers on how to use music to help people with dementia. I never lose sight of the fact that without my many close friends, with whom I've been richly blessed, I would not have survived life's challenges nor shared so many joys with others. My friendships have truly enriched my life beyond imaginable wealth.

My Approach to Building Community

1. Follow Your Passion

I've built community through my passions in life.

I was blessed with several passions in life. The first was music and sharing with others the joy of singing and playing instruments. Following my love of music and finding ways to share it with other people have always provided me solace and energy and led to many lifelong friendships. I have friends from grade school and high school from singing in choruses, from contra dancing in New England and country western dancing in Texas, from choruses I've conducted and many from choruses and choirs I've sung with. A love of travel, nature, of getting to know people from all cultures and cultivating friendships, of helping others, and the enjoyment of being outdoors—all have provided me with ways to build and maintain several types of friendship communities. Now that I'm retired, I made up my own "business card," about my passion for teaching caregivers how to use music to help people with dementia, and I share them liberally everywhere I go. This has greatly widened connections as well.

2. Journaling Helps to Reveal Your Callings

Journaling helps you find your inner guidance.

I have developed many friends, but I live alone and enjoy writing in a journal about the most interesting and perplexing aspects of my life. Sometimes I just write a question I'm struggling with, and then turn my thoughts loose and write down everything that comes to mind. This often helps me find an answer or solution. Writing about times in my life when I was happiest and about what activities were most meaningful or made me feel most fulfilled, helped me see myself more clearly and informed future decisions/directions. I discovered how passionate I was about teaching through my journal writing and that led me to teach choruses at several adult education venues where some of my students became lifelong friends.

3. Learn by Showing Genuine Interest in Others

Virtually all people are my teachers.

I maintain that we all have something to learn from one another—our life experiences teach us myriad ways to navigate our journeys, and the person next to you has gems to share (as do I, as I eventually learned later in life). Striking up a light conversation with acquaintances as well as strangers (in person or on the phone) can lead to interesting and sometimes enlightening discussions, even if you never share your first names. Virtually everyone can share a positive moment, a laugh, an expression of kindness, and some of those sparks bloom into friendships. You never know what you're missing until you put yourself out there, and it's especially fun when positive energy comes back at you. I love discovering how common threads—such as our interests, places we've visited, our tastes in jewelry, favorite cuisines, or music we love—can lead to new social circles with a shared interest and so it goes.

4. Tap Your Local Reference Librarian

Reference librarians are great resources.

A great way to expand your connections and build new communities is to explore favorite topics of interest with the help of a reference librarian. They are often closet Sherlock Holmes types and love to help others sleuth out information—be it topics of your inner passions or places to connect with like-minded others, local social groups, or adult education classes. They can also help search within various budgets—check out free concerts, festivals, museum nights and art exhibits, children's events, and so on—and provide online assistance, such as finding meetups. If you have a favorite or a new passion to explore, like belly dancing or growing container gardens, the library is a great place to start.

5. Pay It Forward by Supporting Others

Most people are starved for positive reinforcement, recognition, and laughter.

This may be truer for certain generations, but I stand by this belief, and it guides many of my interactions, particularly with strangers. I try to use every opportunity that life presents to give away genuine little bits of positivity, however small, such as "What a beautiful ring!" or "You have a great laugh/smile." Whether it's a grocery clerk, the person next to me in line, or the tech support person helping with my billing problem over the phone, I enjoy finding ways to make them laugh and/or express my appreciation for their skills, kindness, and help. Most of these connections aren't meant for friendship, but they may lead to that, and they help others along the way. It's like watering thirsty plants—it adds positivity and beauty to the world and helps counter our common sense of isolation.

6. Stay Open to the World around You

I'm loaded with curiosity.

I have no clue where this comes from—I must I have been born filled with endless curiosity and wonder. I knew music was a passion, but it was really hard to identify a career because I was so interested in all the topics in school. This quest for knowledge and exploration of the world has led me to many new communities—in types of work and different jobs, moving to new places, diversity in friendships, and cultural exposures—all experiences I would never have had without venturing beyond the familiar. Curiosity about individuals led me to become a good and respectful listener, which in turn helps people feel valued and helps me learn about them and whatever else I'm seeking. This inner drive helps me reach out to others and initiate conversation and inevitably propels me into new places (and taking great photos!) and wonderful new friends.

7. Our Extended Family Can Be Our Friends

I've expanded my family into a world of friends!

My birth family has dwindled now to one older sister, but we had a loving, close family all our lives. I always came back home a couple of times a year, but was able to survive the rest of the time because of a strong network of friends. In my quest to live cheaply so I could afford to travel, I moved nearly twenty times in twenty years, and yet in each place I managed to find people who became friends. I now have a chance to go visit them all in my retirement during my frequent road trips around the country—still on a shoestring, but I get to stay with them and we have a wonderful time catching up. Of course, I wasn't able to sustain all my friendships, but there are many who've hung in there with me over some long periods without much communication. These are lifelong, very deep friendships dating back as far as nursery school! They've helped me through two recent (and complicated) knee replacements and numerous and sundry mundane ills and misfortunes. I am grateful every day for my friends and would not have survived without them.

PART FOUR

A Sense OF Belonging

CHAPTER NINE

Taking Action
to Create Community

What Draws Us Out of Our Shell?

As we reflect on the profiles of people in Part Three, we can see how finding our way out of isolation and into our community takes courage, caring, and interest in others. Something very powerful and deep within us can elicit this courage and caring—something strong enough to push us past the barriers that isolate us. Looking deeper, we can see commonalities in their profiles, salient driving forces that led these individuals to participate in their communities and eventually to a greater sense of meaning and belonging.

Through these profiles, and in my own journey out of isolation, I've recognized five common motivating forces—callings—that can pull us into involvement with our communities:

1. Following our caring: Our desire to help others.
2. Following our curiosity: The love of learning and discovery.
3. Following our bliss: Doing what we love.

4. Following our healing: A journey of healing ourselves and others.

5. Following our sense of purpose: A call to make a difference.

Allie, Annie, Robyn, and Paul followed their healing journey to build their communities. Marisa followed her sense of purpose to start an organization to fight breast cancer. Ben and Jan followed their love of learning and discovery. Of course, one driving force can lead to another. For example, Robyn's healing journey after her son's overdose led to her to launch new support groups for other grieving people in her community. Her healing journey became her sense of purpose to help in healing others suffering in similar ways.

One of the greatest commonalities of these profiles is that the issues that isolated these people became the issues that galvanized them to reach out to others. In other words, *what isolates us can become the force that unites us.* Our drive to join others or to gather others can stem from a common isolating force—something that has caused us stigma, pain, or shame can become a mission, a rallying cry to come together. Whether it is illness, addiction, or loss, we find people who have suffered the same thing. Robyn, Allie, Annie, and Paul turned their healing journey into a way of healing others—an authentic, passionate calling.

Ben and Jan longed to share their passion for learning with others. Ben created educational programs for seniors and Jan started music therapy groups.

I was so inspired by the ways these people had created community that I developed a course called *Brave New Friendships* and launched it in June 2018, at an adult education center. To my surprise and delight, it was a hit! I had a large class of people ages twenty to seventy. College students as well as retirees were hungry to find new ways to build friendships, community, and a sense of belonging. It was heartening to observe how the twenty-year-old students shared their social media tips for building community with the baby boomers, and the boomers offered face-to-face conversational tips for the millennials. I witnessed the value of sharing practical wisdom about building community through intergenerational conversations as we benefited from each other's insight on how isolation affects us at different ages.

One of the class participants, twenty-two years old, made a comment that really opened my eyes, "It's strange how much energy and time we put into developing our career networks, but we hardly put that same effort into building our social life! It seems that our social needs are neglected at the expense of building our brands and making money."

Right, I thought. Here, in the US, people spend their energy, time, and money on business or career networking, but what about networking for our *social* happiness—for our personal connections with people who care about *more* than our professional achievements? What about people who care, instead, about us, just as human beings?

Responding to the requests of my students, I created the following mini-toolkit to help us look at our own support networks and opportunities for building our communities and friendships.

Building Your Community

A Mini-Toolkit

Introduction:

REMINDERS FOR BUILDING YOUR COMMUNITY

- **Be in it for the long haul. It usually takes a long time to build solid, face-to-face friendships and partnerships—one or two years or more.** Your great patience and compassion are essential to your commitment of building community, but it's a wise and rewarding investment.

- **Cast a wide net** for meeting new people. Just like job hunting, it takes a lot of "nos" to get to a "yes" when it comes to the right friendship or partnership. Yes, indeed, it *is* a bit of a numbers game. Work those networks by showing up.

- **Stay open-minded and not too fixated on who fits your "tribe."** You might be surprised who welcomes you into his or her world when you aren't trying so hard to find the "right" group to belong to.

- **Be proactive. Reach out to others. Offer your help to others.** This is how you grow your community. Ironically, we gather support by giving support. This is why volunteering is a solid way to build social networks.

- **If you are volunteering as a way to make new friends, keep in mind that serving in a social role can provide you with more opportunities to socialize.** Let your volunteer organizer know you are actively expanding your social network. Otherwise, some volunteer roles can be more solitary than others. (Helping with a mailing may be far less social than helping to host a concert.)

- **It can help to use a calling card when networking, even at social meetups.** It's convenient to hand out a nice card with *at least* your contact info on it so people will remember you, even if you don't have a job. (I know lots of folks using calling cards to build their support networks. I've seen some fun and friendly cards that list interests such as "dog-lover," "indie movie aficionado," "unabashed foodie," and "Mahjong enthusiast" among others.) Of course, standard business cards work well if you prefer to use those.

- **Go to newcomers groups if you are a transplant to a new area—even if you have been in that area for more than a year.** Newcomers groups (or newcomers meetups on Meetup.com) offer ideal ways to meet others who are hungry to build new relationships—often people from out of state or even from a different part of the same state. I know many people who keep going to newcomers' groups for *many* years!

- **If you live alone, you might consider the benefits of house-sharing.** Three or four compatible individuals sharing a home (along with meals, gardening, or carpooling) can create a sense of belonging and connection that goes way beyond being "roomies." (A shared housing website for older women is www.womenlivingincommunity.com.)

- **Please don't be hard on yourself if you are having a difficult time making friends. Many people you meet have very limited time for their social lives or simply are not interested in expanding their networks.** Americans typically spend less time investing in their social networks than in their business or professional networks. Most people put their social lives on the back burner while dealing with more immediate situations in the front burners of their lives. Many people would love to build new friendships or enhance their social life but just don't have the time, energy, or focus.

- **Try not to take it personally (or overthink it) when people turn down your invitation to get together.** Many people might not be interested in developing a new friendship (for many reasons that may have nothing to do with you as a person).

- **People might flake on you or just suddenly disappear.** Those who join you for one or two gatherings still might back out of visiting with you on an ongoing basis. Some might even disappear without a word. Again, don't take this personally. Some people only want a little companionship from time to time but don't really want to develop an ongoing friendship (and feel too awkward to say anything for fear of letting you down). Please give yourself lots of compassion and respect for taking the risk of trying a new friendship, and don't give up on searching for another friendship. Keep moving forward.

- **Seek the support of counseling, ministry, a support group, or a helpline if you are feeling overwhelmed or despondent about building your community.** I'd like to add what one of our contributors, Pam Blunt, a psychotherapist, said in her profile, "If we don't have much social interaction, self-critical voices can find fertile ground inside our minds." Remember that we need human interaction to face loneliness and isolation, including professional support if we lack social support. Support is always out there, and you are not alone.

Part 1.

EXERCISES TO BUILD YOUR COMMUNITY

The following guided exercises offer ways to reflect on your current social supports. All of your networks can build a social safety net of support. How might you expand your networks and create community?

A. Mapping My Support Networks

EMOTIONAL
SUPPORT
People We Confide In
Feeling Safe, Confidential,
Private, Empathic,
Good Listeners,
Meaningful Conversations,
We Can Be Vulnerable,
Acceptance, Respect,
Comfort

AFFILIATIVE
SUPPORT
Groups We Join
Common Interests,
Common Causes,
Purposeful Activities,
Meaningful Activities,
Creative Activities,
Passions, Callings,
Recreation, Hobbies,
Fun Stuff

**The Wider
Community**
Helplines, Hotlines, Warmlines,
Support Groups,
Twelve-Step Groups,
Counseling, Coaching,
Meetups, Associations,
Clubs, Volunteering,
Serving Causes, Classes,
Study Groups, Travel,
Faith-Based Communities,
Advocacy, Social Action

TANGIBLE
SUPPORT
People Who Assist Us
Hands-On Support,
Errands, Shopping,
Home Care, Cleaning,
Moving, Caregiver
Support, Transportation,
Assist with Doctor
Visits, Financial Aid,
Food Aid

KNOWLEDGE
SUPPORT
People with Knowledge
People with Experience
(Have "Been Through It"
Before You), Resources,
Advice, Ideas,
Facts, Research,
Studies

B. An Inventory of My Support Networks

Write down the first names of supportive people in your life. Who is "there" for you? It's fine to list the same person in more than one support network. Include online communities as well as offline communities. You are taking a wide inventory of the people and groups in your life who provide a sense of belonging.

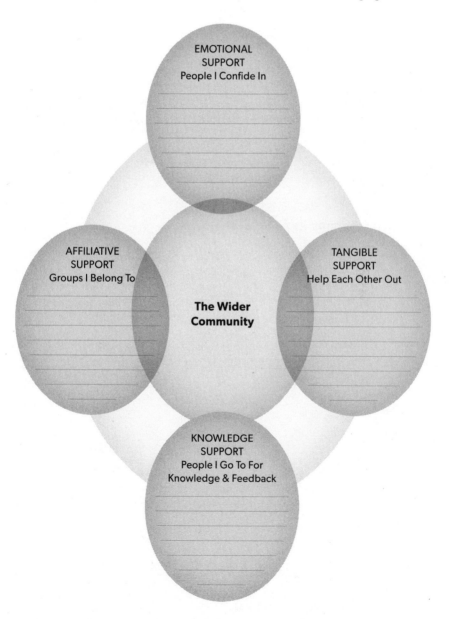

C. Where Does My Social Support Come From (online and face-to-face)?

EMOTIONAL SUPPORT: People I confide in (and feel safe with)

_____

_____

_____

> *Do I need to find other people for emotional support?*

Next Step: _____

TANGIBLE SUPPORT: People who help out (and I help them, too)

_____

_____

_____

> *Do I need to expand my help-each-other-out team?*

Next Step: _____

KNOWLEDGE SUPPORT: People I go to for knowledge, information, & feedback

_____

_____

_____

> *Do I need to look for more knowledge or contacts?*

Next Step: _____

AFFILIATIVE SUPPORT: Groups I belong to (volunteering, meetups, associations, clubs)

_____

_____

_____

> *Do I need to try out more groups?*

Next Step: _____

Part 2.
WHAT IT TAKES TO GET ME OFF THE COUCH AND OUT THE DOOR TO MEET PEOPLE

Where did you meet friendly people (in person) over the past few years?

Think of **three settings** where you met friendly people. (Examples: Dinner party, meetup, athletic event, arts event, a class, volunteering, outdoor activity, spiritual retreat, support group, recovery group.)

_____

_____

_____

_____

What activities did you enjoy with friendly people over the past few years?

(Examples: Eating, playing golf, cheering for a ball game, art shows, sailing, birdwatching, mentoring kids, sightseeing.) Name **three activities** you were enjoying when you met friendly people over the past few years.

_____

_____

_____

_____

Who are the most enjoyable, warm, and interesting people you have spent time with over the past few years?

List **three people** and **three qualities** you like about each of them.

PERSON: _____

Personal Qualities: _____

PERSON: _____

Personal Qualities: _____

PERSON: _____

Personal Qualities: _____

Based on the positive experiences you've listed above, how would you sum up your best bets for new opportunities to make friends?

Where are your best locations or settings for meeting friendly and interesting people?

_____   _____   _____

_____   _____   _____

What are your best activities for meeting friendly and interesting people?

_____   _____   _____

_____   _____   _____

Who are the types of people you're seeking to meet—their qualities and values?

_____   _____   _____

_____   _____   _____

Part 3.
GRATITUDE FOR PEOPLE WHO'VE SUPPORTED ME IN MY LIFE

One of the best ways to appreciate how we've been supported by others is to do a simple gratitude exercise. Take a few minutes to remember the times people reached out to you. Feeling gratitude for others is vital for attaining the strength and hope we need to keep reaching out to others. Just knowing how we have been supported reassures us that people have "been there" for us. And furthermore, naming what we're grateful for helps us identify the kinds of people we seek for building friendships and community.

In this gratitude exercise, list five different experiences of when someone supported you or went out of his or her way to help you, even when you weren't expecting it. Reflect on the qualities of the person who helped you, as well as the ways those actions helped you.

I am grateful for these five experiences of being supported by others:

1: _____

_____

_____

2: _____

_____

_____

3: _____

_____

_____

4: _____

_____

5: _____

What did I learn from these experiences of being supported?

What are the qualities of the people who supported me?

What were their values?

What are the qualities and values that I possess for supporting others?

Part 4.

WAYS TO CONNECT WITH OLD CONNECTIONS— THEY'RE OUT THERE SOMEWHERE

Rediscovering people from past associations can help us rebuild our support networks and tap into old friendships. Here are some ways to look for people we knew in the past:

- Alumni associations
- High school reunions
- Facebook and LinkedIn
- High school yearbooks
- Old address books (from the 1980s, 1990s, 2000s)
- Old journals and notebooks
- Boxes of memorabilia and old letters
- Old email addresses

List your ideas for finding old friends or "long-lost cousins."

_____

_____

_____

_____

_____

_____

Part 5.

DO I KNOW ANYONE WHO IS GREAT AT BUILDING FRIENDSHIPS AND COMMUNITY?

(Real-life Role Models of Savvy Networkers and Community-Builders)

We might know a smart, socially adept networker who might teach us a few tips. Someone around us might have done a brilliant job of growing a strong circle of friends and community, even after a major life change and having to start over. We might reach out to our "role models" of community-building and see what they could share with us. Who knows—they might appreciate the opportunity to share what they know!

So, ask around.

Even though I'm in my sixties, I have chatted with savvy twenty-somethings as well as widowed women in their seventies who've given me tips on where to find interesting groups. No one has the last word on how to build community, but definitely some wise people are out there to happily share their suggestions.

Part 6.

IN PRAISE OF VOLUNTEERING

Of all the ways I've witnessed people who broke out of isolation and became happily involved in their communities, I can't say enough about the benefits of volunteering. Being a volunteer for a cause or organization is an excellent way to build solid friendships because we have the structure and regularity in our lives to make bonds with people volunteering with us. A volunteer job is quite different than working at a fast-paced, competitive workplace because people tend to feel a bit more relaxed and personable in a volunteer setting. We are there because we *want* to be there and are open to meeting new people. In my work as a rehabilitation counselor for twenty-two years, I've witnessed how volunteering jobs worked wonders for my clients who were healing from isolation and loneliness. When contributing to our communities by spending our free time with others, the most withdrawn and marginalized people may take bold leaps of faith and break through social barriers and stigma.

Many volunteer opportunities can be found at the following organizations:

- Habitat for Humanity
- American Red Cross
- Special Olympics
- National Park Service
- YMCA and YWCA
- Jewish Federation
- Easter Seals (summer camps)
- General Federation of Women's Clubs
- Audubon Society
- American Cancer Society
- Sierra Club
- Peace Corps
- Girl Scouts of America and Boy Scouts of America
- Big Sisters and Big Brothers of America
- Americorps and VISTA
- OSHER Lifelong Learning Centers (OLLI)
- Doctors without Borders

And here are popular local volunteer ideas:

- Public library
- Hospice
- Art museum or historical museum
- Food pantry
- Animal rescue shelters
- Retirement communities
- Senior centers
- Hospitals, cancer centers, other associations for treatment of diseases
- Agencies for people with disabilities
- Local church, synagogue, temple
- Domestic violence shelter or women's shelter
- Literacy programs
- Community gardens
- Parks and playgrounds

Part 7.

MANY WAYS TO MAKE NEW FRIENDS AND BUILD COMMUNITY

Check any of these pursuits that spark your interest. What energizes you?

- **Serving Others**

  - Volunteering for an organization or cause
  - Helping your neighbors
  - Helping your friends and family members
  - Helping your colleagues/coworkers

  - Contributing to websites: your ideas, suggestions, stories, comments
  - Promoting businesses, projects, initiatives that help others
  - Other: _____

- **Learning with Others and Teaching Others**

  - Taking classes at community education centers, colleges, other centers
  - Learning new skills in more informal ways (watching how other people do things)
  - Going on tours, even in your local community (historic sites, gardens, museums)

  - Traveling and exploring
  - Retreats
  - Discussion groups
  - Book clubs
  - Teaching classes on a topic you love
  - Research and study groups (or participating in a study)
  - Other: _____

- **Creating with Others**

  - Joining others in a creative project or mission (online or offline)

  - Going to support groups that involve creative projects

- Sharing your creations in galleries, art shows, craft shows
- Crafting with a meetup
- Art activities with a meetup
- Playing a musical instrument with a group or meetup
- Singing in a choir or a band
- Theater groups
- Writing projects or groups or meetups
- Film making and production with a group
- Dance groups (ballroom dancing, country/square dancing, folk dancing, improv)
- Decorating spaces with others
- Inventing new products
- Other: _____

- **Enterprising with Others**
  - Starting a business or nonprofit based on your passion
  - Helping others promote their new products or businesses
  - Investing in a new venture that builds community, fundraising
  - Being on a board for a nonprofit
  - Other: _____

- **Advocacy with Others**
  - Joining a political campaign
  - Working with an organization or cause
  - Starting an organization or group for a cause
  - Other: _____

- **Sports/Athletic/Fitness Events with Others:**
  - Going to games with friends or a group
  - Being part of a team
  - Being a member of a gym, exercise studio, or yoga studio
  - Running or being in a marathon
  - Special Olympics
  - Paralympic Games
  - Being a member of a fan club or meetup
  - Other: _____

- **Keeping the Faith with Others (Spiritual and Religious Activities)**

  - Being in a congregation or a member of a church, synagogue, temple, mosque
  - Joining in social events at your religious or spiritual community
  - Retreats (prayer retreats, meditation retreats, other)
  - Celebrations, rituals, life passages
  - Discussion groups
  - Other: _____

- **Animals and Nature with Others**

  - Being a part of a group for animal lovers (dogs, cats, horses, birds)
  - Participating in events that involve animals (dog shows, cat shows, equestrian events)
  - Birdwatching events
  - Being active with programs for animal-assisted therapies
  - Being active with a community gardening project
  - Going to garden events or clubs
  - Outdoor activities (kayaking, canoeing, hiking, climbing, kite-flying)
  - Walking with friends and loved ones
  - Being a member of an environmental protection group
  - Other: _____

- **Socializing with Others for Fun**

  - Food-related meetups at restaurants
  - Trivia nights
  - Comedy clubs
  - Karaoke fun
  - Open mic nights
  - Card game groups (bridge, poker, other)
  - Game nights
  - Festivals
  - Concerts
  - Parties (hosting as well as attending)
  - Socials, fun meetups
  - Other: _____

Self-Reflection:

What activities are most likely to bring you out of your shell?

_____

_____

_____

What social activities give you a sense of purpose or meaning?

_____

_____

_____

What activities do you think will be most productive for meeting like-minded people?

_____

_____

_____

What kinds of environments are best for meeting new people?

(In other words, how would you describe being "in your element?")

_____

_____

_____

Reflecting on your motivating forces—callings—for building community, which of these forces draw you out of your shell? (We can have more than one driving force— maybe all of these.)

1. Following my caring: A desire to help others.

2. Following my curiosity: The love of learning and discovery.

3. Following my bliss: Doing what I love.

4. Following my healing: A journey of healing myself and others.

5. Following my sense of purpose: A call to make a difference.

What is your calling (or callings) for building friendships, community, and a sense of belonging?

_____

_____

_____

_____

_____

_____

_____

_____

_____

CHAPTER TEN

400 Friends and a Few to Count On

Full Circle: After My Surgery, March 2019

On the last day of winter, March 19, 2019, at Massachusetts General Hospital in Boston, I underwent surgery for a small thyroid cancer, as well as a benign tumor in my diseased parathyroid glands. Wiped out, sore, lacking much of a voice, unable to swallow much food, and without being able to turn my head or drive, I relied on a small circle of friends to do the heavy lifting. One friend, Rita, stood by my side at the hospital and at home. She served as my driver, my secretary, my activities therapist, and my supplier of medicines and the vital calcium and other supplements I needed (now that my parathyroid functions were zapped.) It took a good ten days before I could eat semisolid food, shower, dress, and return to driving short distances.

After a week of recovery, as my voice became stronger and the soreness wore away, Rita and I enjoyed hours of conversation, reminiscing about being roommates in her tiny apartment when I had first moved to Boston. Exactly six years earlier, in March 2013, I'd arrived at her door with my single carload of belongings, no furniture except a white wicker chair and a bookcase. She recalled how I ran to multiple food pantries for my groceries and scraped by without my medicine, so I would have enough money for gas to get to my new job. I'd barely managed to pay her my share of the rent.

"Rita, I was a refugee from Maine. I told you I moved to Mass to save my ass."

Rita nodded slowly, thinking hard. "Oh God, I felt so bad for you. You were so broke and so worn out. I kept the rent for your room as affordable as I could."

I loved her broad Minnesota accent. Rita had moved to Boston from Minneapolis with her husband eighteen years earlier. But by the time I arrived at her apartment, she had been divorced for a year, scraping by as I was, juggling an outsourcing business of her own around a full-time job as an office manager for a solar engineering company. She was on the phone constantly, if not with her clients, then with her mom from Minneapolis, who checked in every evening around 7:00 p.m. Rita always worked through her meals, hurriedly eating her take-out salads standing at her kitchen counter while talking on her speaker phone. She typically worked up to 10:00 p.m., until she all but crawled into bed.

"All you did was work your tail off, Rita. I hardly saw you."

"And good thing you never saw me, because I was a bitch right after my divorce," she chuckled.

"I just thought you were a workaholic and kept my distance."

"And I thought you were a loner who just wanted to stay in her room and watch Netflix every night."

"I think the only time we ever socialized was when Ana and Marco invited us to join them downstairs."

"They were most generous people—the sweetest people I've ever met. We did have fun with them, didn't we?"

We recalled the fleeting little joys of joining our neighbors downstairs during the years we lived together. In the apartment right below us, Rita had sparked a tender friendship with an elderly couple from Bulgaria, Ana and Marco, who were more than ecstatic for us to join them for home-baked desserts and glasses of port. On a few Sunday evenings we gathered, squeezing around Ana's kitchen table alongside the Brazilian neighbors from across the hall and our Italian landlord, who popped in. We eagerly shared photos from our phones of the people and places we loved far away, cheerfully chatting, often light-heartedly interrupting each other in a cacophony of show-and-tell storytelling. We were all transplants to Boston from around the world living together in our modest, three-story brick building on Arlington Road.

Ana and Rita had developed a surrogate mother-daughter relationship. She helped Ana with her bookkeeping, running errands, and dumping her trash, chatting constantly while they multitasked. Every Saturday night Ana invited her to dinner, begging her, "You need to have fun for a change and stop working so much!" Rita usually turned down her invitation, but Ana insisted on dropping off warm covered dishes full of huge helpings, which Rita shared with me.

Rita tenderly recollected, "Ana and Marco were my only friends that year after my divorce. It was so easy having them right downstairs as my go-to Mom and Dad. They needed me and I needed them. We were perfect for each other."

We remembered how, other than those few gatherings with Ana and Marco, we had kept our lives very much apart. It wasn't until Rita had moved out to Northampton in the western part of the state that we began a real friendship. Without the pressure and worry of renting a room as her tenant, I was able to chat with her more casually. I even took on some per diem work to help her out in a pinch with her fast-growing medical billing business.

"I thought you were headed back to Minnesota after I moved out. You always said you hated Massachusetts—hated the 'Massholes,' those rude, crazy drivers pushing you off the road, how crowded it was here, how impatient everyone was. I was surprised you stayed in Massachusetts and settled in Northampton."

"Actually, I've become a Masshole driver myself—I don't take shit from anyone," Rita snickered. "Massachusetts has rubbed off on me in a good way. I'm not that nice, reserved gal from Minnesota anymore—you betcha. I'm a full, fledged Masshole and I'm *wicked* proud!"

We laughed and bantered with fake (awful) Boston accents, trying to sound tough.

"Yeah, Massachusetts has rubbed off well on me, too. Strange how I fit in here better than anywhere else. Certainly, better than my home state. Back in Virginia, people were mostly outgoing and friendly, full of Southern hospitality. But hospitality and social graciousness didn't always mean genuine friendship. It's Southern culture—being welcoming and inviting is very important—but people have *very* high standards for those niceties. You're supposed to be able to read those social cues and little nuances, but I truly never could. I flunked Southern Culture 101 because I was too damn honest, open, intense, awkward. I was clueless about how to play it. I never really learned those social cues because I broke away from my family at a young age—a dark history I don't talk about—so I hunted for friends to be my family. Of course, starving to belong somewhere was a setup for tragedy. I often mistook invitations to social events as signs of true friendship, as real belonging. I was such a sucker, confusing friendliness with friendship. At least here in Boston, as a failed Southerner, I know where I stand—and that's a relief! I don't have to guess who my real friends are."

"You're right. Not much fake friendliness around here. People don't invite you to stuff unless they genuinely like you. You can tell right away if someone really means to be your friend or, otherwise, people blow you off very early in the conversation. But I'm curious—when did you decide to cut your ties with Virginia?"

Rita reassured me it was okay to keep going with my sad, lonely story. "You know, Rita, before I moved to Boston, back in June 2012, I thought I still had a couple of friends back in Virginia. I realized I'd outgrown Maine after fourteen years of a quiet, rural life as my three friends there had either disappeared, moved on, or just gotten too busy with their grandkids. It seemed I had no one left in Maine anymore—where should I go? As a last resort, I figured I'd return to my home state of Virginia and check out the scene to see how my old friends were doing. I honestly told them I just didn't know where I belonged anymore and humbly asked if they thought I'd fit back in to their lives. But, oh my God—I think my vulnerability scared those old friends away! Sure enough, I found out that they had gossiped behind my back about how fragile and needy I was."

Rita listened closely. "So, you flat-out told them you needed them after being away for fourteen years? You actually told them that all your friends in Maine had disappeared? Oh, dear—Val, they must have felt really awkward. Maybe they freaked out. So, are you *sure* they said you were fragile? Or did you just assume they said that?"

"Yes, one friend *did* tell me to my face—that, indeed, most of my friends had *always* thought I was fragile—but they 'didn't have the heart to tell me.'"

"That's a shitty thing to find out. But at least you found out the truth."

"You know, Rita, how we've talked about those great books that tell us it's so beautiful to be vulnerable? How we need to be brave and to tell the truth and be authentic and all that stuff? Well, showing our vulnerability and loneliness only works with certain people and in certain places and at certain times. God forbid you don't have a single family member or a single friend to be vulnerable with! God help you if people say you're needy when you are truly in need of their caring and love. Rita, I tell you there is nothing that hurts more than being told how needy and fragile we are! Damn those books that preach about being vulnerable when we don't have *anyone* to be vulnerable *with*!"

Rita noticed I was holding back tears. "Val, those books weren't meant for you. Those books weren't meant for people who don't have anyone to turn to. Those books weren't meant for people who don't have friends or family to count on."

"Damn right." I wiped my eyes.

Intrigued, Rita continued thinking out loud. "Being vulnerable in our culture is risky. We have to be very careful who we open up to or else we will be judged as needy. I find it ironic that showing our vulnerability can be helpful for people who *already* have support, but it can be devastating for people who are truly alone without anyone to talk to—others run from them. It's really sad how the people who need us the most are the ones who scare us away."

"Yeah, you get it, Rita. When people without social support are looking for friends or partners, they need to be careful to hide their vulnerability and not let a bit of that loneliness show—so people don't think you'll latch onto them. People who've always had social support don't understand how hard it is for people who don't have that support. It's easier for folks who already have a supportive family and friends to make new friends or find partners because it's less of a risk for them and they're not as exposed—their support system is like having shock absorbers that buffer the rejection and the judgment of others. Plus, if you have loved ones in your life, then you have someone to talk about besides yourself, so you appear more normal—you have your grandkid's photos, your spouse's hobbies, or your sister's business to chat about. Heaven help us if we have no one to talk about (except our cat or ourselves) and we are out there trying to make friends. We could scare off someone in a heartbeat if they can see how isolated we really are."

"So, Val, people judged you as needy and fragile when you admitted you were lonely and needed friends. But to tell you the truth—*I* don't see you as fragile."

"Even when I landed on your doorstep six years ago? I didn't have anyone. I was practically homeless. I looked like a bag lady."

"Like I said, you *did* look worn out and raw. Sure, you were a tad irritable and overwhelmed. But what I liked about you was that you were so damn hopeful. You said you were excited to start over again in Boston. That you loved Boston, even though you hardly knew anyone. I admired your faith. And I believed you were going to do well here because you were so in love with the place!"

"Thank you . . . You know, I *was* so excited to start over—you're right."

"You made the right choice moving to Boston. Mass really has saved your ass."

"Thank God. It turns out I do prefer the northeastern US. People are more direct here. If someone thinks I'm looking fragile, they would tell me, 'You look like crap today.' I know this is true because one day one of my coworkers *did* tell me that. I sincerely thanked her for letting me know and assured her I was having an awful day. But it felt good just to be open about it and nip it in the bud."

"Val," she sighed. "I never felt that I belonged in Minnesota, and when my ex left me stranded after following him to Boston, I, too, was lost and isolated. Thank God for Ana and Marco downstairs, but they were so much older than I. Fortunately, my business not only kept me sane, but I could network with it and make new friends along the way. I'm certain that my real family is my circle of friends in Massachusetts, but it also took me six years. Some friends are transplants from other states who came here, just like you, with old baggage and old luggage. It's taken a damn long time to believe my home was really here, but I've got a few good friends to prove it!"

"As do I," I chimed in. "We've both done well for two transplants who never fit in anywhere else."

"Hey, you know, I've always wondered why you picked Boston to move to. After you decided to leave Maine and decided you'd never return to Virginia—why Boston?"

"I will never forget that Sunday in June back in 2012, when I came to Boston on a whim—it was all because I wanted to see a particular movie! Three weeks after my surgery in Maine for a hysterectomy, I'd been going stir crazy recovering at home. I was in a major funk—having the nastiest, biggest pity party of my life because my friends had let me down me in Virginia *and* my friends had disappeared in Maine. Finally, to snap out of my funk, I craved going out to see a movie called *Moonrise Kingdom,* the latest from one of my favorite directors, Wes Anderson. I had intended to see it in Portland, but unfortunately it wasn't opening there for another month. I noticed when I searched online that it was already playing in Boston. I figured, why not hop on the train for a fun day's outing? So, I went to Boston, saw this sweet, quirky movie about two lonely twelve-year-old misfits who found each other and fell in love. The movie's message was the perfect lift I needed: Yes, misfits could find each other if we never give up. Basking in the glow of the movie, I strolled down Tremont Street, wandered through the Common, and even did a bit of the Freedom Trail. I popped into a pub and had a beer and some homemade chili, and watched a Red Sox game on the wide screen along with the locals. I enjoyed the buzzy, happy vibe. People were certainly easier to chat with than in Maine, where folks are more reserved. So, in short, I was a tourist for a beautiful day in June and had a blast in Beantown. On the train back to Portland, I began to imagine myself living in Boston."

"Wow . . . so it all started with a movie. I think I would have traveled two hours to see a Wes Anderson movie. That's amazing."

"Right! Wes Anderson was my inspiration—thanks, Wes! Your wonderful movie got me off the sofa, out the door, out of my funk, and off to Boston."

We laughed. We savored the idea that following our bliss, venturing out to a movie, or a concert or a ball game, was a sure way to bust out of our blues. But was following our bliss a sound reason for making such a major life decision as moving to a new city? I had only visited Boston for one day as a tourist, going to touristy sites.

"It seems strange, Rita, that I knew in my gut I wanted to move to Boston, even after one day of sightseeing. But at that time, I had nothing to lose and nothing to keep me anywhere. I had no clue where I belonged anymore. Why not try something entirely different? And I knew Boston offered far more job opportunities than Maine. Why not go for it?"

Rita smiled with an "aha" look in her eyes. "And then you contacted your long-lost ex-cousin-in-law, Sandra, the one and only person you knew in Boston who might give you some tips on moving and, voilà, she told you I was looking for a roommate. So you ended up with me when you landed here!"

"And thank God I met you!"

Rita popped out of the room to get a couple of cans of ginger ale, poured them, and handed me an icy cold glass. She sat down by my window in my old wicker chair (the one I'd schlepped from Virginia to Maine and to Boston for twenty years) as the evening sun glowed around her. She sipped her drink, and paused, smiling knowingly.

"You know, when I was downstairs a minute ago, I just remembered something: You told me back in 2012 how no one had helped you after your surgery in Maine. How you had no one to call for support. You were stranded, alone, right after your hysterectomy. But that was seven years ago. Now . . . look at how different your life is after *this* surgery. You have friends all around you helping out. You have get-well cards coming in and pink tulips delivered and phone calls and texts and Facebook posts—everyone's been so kind. And you have me right here with you."

I suddenly realized Rita had witnessed my long journey from the get-go when I landed in Boston. Her words reassured me that my sad, lonely story had turned around. I had come full circle: The aftermath of my surgery in spring 2019 was nothing like the aftermath of my surgery of spring 2012. My entire world had changed after living in Boston for six years. It had taken every single day of those years to build those friendships, and my God, did those years of community-building, self-advocating, self-compassion, and *patience* pay off! What a difference a few true-blue friends can make.

"Rita, I'm so blessed to have you here as a witness to my story. I'm not only fortunate to have you here to take care of me after surgery, but you've seen how much my world has changed. And look—we've both come full circle."

We both became a little teary. We had worked hard and made many sacrifices to rebuild our lives in Massachusetts. We toasted with our ginger ales, celebrating how far we'd come and that we belonged here, not by simply hunting for a place to belong, but by creating our belonging here.

After two more days of recovery from my surgery, I was well on the mend and Rita packed her luggage to return to Northampton. I helped Rita shove her luggage into the back of her car and gave her a long hug.

She sat at her wheel and tweaked her GPS settings. "It only takes an hour and a half to get to Northampton. I'll be okay."

"Don't you dare be texting until you get back to Northampton."

"I promise. Remember, I've become a good Masshole driver now."

We laughed and Rita carefully backed out of the driveway and turned west. I sat on my porch and looked up to the soft, pale blue sky and across the white picket fences and the small white houses crowded together on my winding street. A patch of light green grass glowed amid the melting ribbons of snow throughout my yard. Two chickadees appeared to be madly in love with each other, hopping between the branches of pine trees and back to the fence, chasing each other and chatting nonstop.

A robin landed on the fence and the chickadees flew away. Spring was here. I was cancer-free, and I had a few loving friends like Rita to count on. What more did I need? I could finally bid farewell to my long, sad story of isolation.

Loving Where We Live

I sat down at my desk to reacquaint myself with all my email and snail mail, getting back on track with my normal responsibilities after recovering from my surgery. I opened many get-well cards among my sky-high pile of medical bills. I spread the bright pink, yellow, and green cards across my window sill, displaying each one with a bit of reverence, as if on an altar. Inside the cards were invitations. One of my friends, Barbara, invited me to join her at Walden Pond for a showing of her photography. My old friend in Maine, Becky, invited me to meet her grandchild at a party at her gazebo. Another friend in Maine asked if I would join her for a walk on Higgins Beach in late April. Another in Massachusetts was eager for me to join her to hear her fiancé sing with his band at a pub in Westborough. Another invited me to see her new apartment in New York City.

It suddenly occurred to me that every one of my friends loved where they lived and were fully engaged in their communities. They wanted to share their favorite spots, at kitchen tables, on porches, outdoor cafes, under trees, by ponds, in parks, in gazebos, on beaches. They all had found their special places where they shined in their own element. They all needed their go-to places as much as they needed their go-to people. As the snow melted throughout New England, and the grass and trees began to "green up," my friends, energized and bursting out of their winter hibernation, were more than happy to celebrate spring with gatherings of all sorts.

I reflected on how important it is to love where we live and what my friend Rita had told me—that indeed, I had fallen in love with Boston long before I ever made friends here. Before any relationships developed, I enjoyed a sense of the community buzzing around me, at least vicariously, by investing in and nurturing my sense of place—much like a garden that takes tending. Fascinated in my new city, beginning on that glorious Sunday in June when I came to see a Wes Anderson movie and explored Boston Common and the Freedom Trail, my shyness and fear took a back seat, allowing my curiosity to take over. I easily asked questions about the stories behind popular historic destinations and watering holes and bantered with locals as well as tourists. I ventured on foot to the neighboring towns of Concord, Cambridge, or Newton, and the area grew on me. I was unabashedly enchanted by so much history, so many colleges and universities, the bustling, walkable towns, the passion for learning, students from ages eighteen to eighty, from all around the world coming to the area because of their callings. My love for my new metropolitan area served as a force that drew me out of my grief for the relationships I had lost, out of my shame of being alone, and out of isolation.

Long before my encounter with my first friend in Boston, Barbara Olson, I had already fallen in love with Walden Pond when I was seventeen, reading about this beloved sanctuary in my twelfth-grade English class. It was hardly a surprise that my first words with Barbara at the lunch counter at that little café on Main Street would be about Henry David Thoreau. Passionate about his work and his life, Barbara chatted happily with me about volunteering at his home and eagerly welcomed me to join her on a tour. Indeed, our friendship was sparked by our mutual passion for Walden Pond.

This love of place was the source of the bliss, the curiosity, and the caring that pulled me out of myself and into my new community. I was truly a pilgrim landing in Massachusetts in 2012, hardly knowing anyone, arriving after fifty years of never fitting in with people anywhere else. I will audaciously state that I felt a kinship with the earlier pilgrims as well as the immigrants still coming, though certainly more persecuted, judged, and shunned than I.

My friends have become the family I chose, and Boston has become the home I created. My book is my story of how my dream came true. Others have chimed in and celebrated with me how we broke free from the grip of isolation and followed our callings:

We followed our caring, and that made us brave.
We followed our curiosity, and that made us brave.
We followed our bliss, and that made us brave.
We followed our healing, and that made us brave.
We followed our sense of purpose, and that made us brave.

And through our callings, we befriended the loneliness inside us as well as the loneliness outside us, as one and the same. We didn't simply hunt for friends, for partners, for soulmates, for surrogate families. Instead, we *invited* people to join what called us out of ourselves, at least for the moment. It could have been a whim, say, a Wes Anderson movie or the music of a concert in the park or a historic tour of Walden Pond or a story told by guests at a party.

We all need "conversation pieces," points of interest, passions, missions, projects, sights that take our breath away—what breaks the ice and gets us chatting and reaching out to one another, long before a friendship or romance can grow. But even in our own backyards, fleeting, odd, or amazing things will surprise us and get us talking, out of the blue, with a stranger.

Every single encounter in our community, from standing in line at the grocery store to walking our dog in a park, is an opportunity to break out of isolation. Our sense of place and belonging can grow, like any other relationship, when we reach out, pay it forward, and give support to those around us. As long as we care about others, right in the communities we live in, we can free ourselves from the insidious pull of isolation.

It's downright magical when people reach out to us on days we feel invisible. Suddenly we are seen and the whole world opens up to welcome us. Every day we have the power to create little sanctuaries of belonging with one another.

Let's not shy away.

PART FIVE

Appendix

Fighting the
Epidemic of Loneliness
A Resource Guide

INITIATIVES AND ORGANIZATIONS TACKLING LONELINESS

• **Sidewalk Talk Community Listening Project**

www.sidewalktalksf.com

"Our mission is to nurture human connection by teaching and practicing heart-centered listening in public spaces," their website boldly states. Started in San Francisco, California, this street initiative is active in most states around the US—in fifty cities and growing also in twelve countries. Volunteers trained to listen empathically sit on sidewalks with chairs in public places so people can conveniently sit down to talk about what is on their minds. This fast-growing project is also a great way to volunteer directly for fighting to end loneliness—right in your own community.

Founder: Traci Ruble

- **Connect2Affect (AARP)**

www.connect2affect.org

Developed for people over fifty, this website is an ideal, user-friendly source for fighting social isolation, and helps people get more involved in their communities. It is a wonderful resource for learning about isolation and loneliness. This AARP initiative publishes many studies and opens our eyes with evidenced-based suggestions for fighting loneliness. Because this website is so informative and helpful, I highly recommend that millennials as well as boomers check it out for ideas on how to build community and break out of isolation.

- **The Unlonely Project, Foundation for Art and Healing**

https://artandhealing.org/unlonely-overview/

The Unlonely Project hosts a film festival featuring themes of loneliness, and many videos can be viewed on their website. Their site also provides excellent reporting on research about isolation and loneliness, and also informs us about conferences and symposiums on fighting social isolation nationwide. The latest in news and media about loneliness is here.

Founder: Jeremy Nobel, MD, MPH

- **The Caring Collaborative (Part of the Transition Network)**

https://www.thetransitionnetwork.org/connect-caring-collaborative/

The Transition Network's Caring Collaborative is a constellation of women, organized by neighborhood in some chapters, providing local assistance and peer support, and establishing lasting bonds. This collaborative provides "neighbor-to-neighbor" genuine caring and help. The volunteers offer face-to-face "help insurance." People receive hands-on assistance during times of surgery, recovery, and other medical interventions. Launched in New York under a grant from the NYS Health Foundation, the model was designed so it could be replicated nationwide. The Caring Collaborative is growing and now has chapters in twelve states.

• Caring Bridge

www.caringbridge.org

CaringBridge is a nonprofit organization designed to help rally support for a loved one during a medical journey, often to plan for hands-on assistance before and after surgery. A family member or friend going through medical procedures can create a webpage that is used to coordinate the support of family and friends across a wide network—an excellent way to organize and plan care with a circle of supportive people. This helps to keep loved ones updated about the progress of the patient and to schedule visits and assistance for the patient once in recovery at home. CaringBridge helps to fight the isolation of patients by bringing people together through the patient's webpage and online journaling. CaringBridge is now in 235 countries around the world.

• Campaign to End Loneliness, United Kingdom

https://www.campaigntoendloneliness.org/

Their mission is to increase awareness of loneliness and to address the underlying causes of loneliness in older individuals throughout the United Kingdom. They host the "world's largest conference dedicated to tackling loneliness," according to their website. This campaign began with a "befriending" initiative to train staff and volunteers to provide companionship to isolated adults. This website offers comprehensive as well as inspiring research and resources for fighting loneliness and building community.

- **Jo Cox Commission on Loneliness, United Kingdom**

www.jocoxfoundation.org/loneliness_commission

In January 2018, the UK appointed their own Minister of Loneliness to lead the Jo Cox Commission on Loneliness. Mims Davies recently (May 2019) took over the position of Minister of Loneliness after Tracey Crouch served for a year. This position was created when Britain recognized how loneliness had become a serious health hazard. Former Prime Minister, Theresa May, deemed loneliness "a sad reality of modern life." Mims Davies is now calling for funding to help families afford to take their elder loved ones on vacations and holidays. The Minister of Loneliness is the head of the Jo Cox Commission on Loneliness.

- **MUSH, United Kingdom**

https://letsmush.com/

In the United Kingdom, there is an app for mothers of young children to build social networks and organize small groups for chatting and connecting. "An easy and fun way for mums to find friends."
Cofounders: Sarah Hesz, Katie Massie-Taylor

- **Togetherness Program (CareMore Health, California)**

www.caremore.com

Robin Caruso, LCSW, Togetherness Officer at CareMore, leads a clinical initiative to reach out to seniors to tackle loneliness and isolation throughout eight states. This has helped link seniors to local community resources and also to bring seniors together who are in similar life situations.

- **Health Leads (Partnering with medical centers in Massachusetts, California, and growing to other states)**

www.healthleadsusa.org

Health Leads is focused on social needs interventions in hospitals and clinics as well as linking patients to local community resources. Designed to serve isolated, low-income, and disenfranchised patients without family, friends, or resources to support them, the Health Leads data base (partnering with United Way and 2-1-1 systems combined) can be accessed by doctors, nurses, or social workers when a patient in their care needs referrals to local resources. Health Leads also provides assessments for medical providers to better identify isolated and underserved individuals and guides providers in ways to link these patients and activate local support services. United Way and 2-1-1 have both shared their databases and other innovative software to connect resources for isolated patients.

- **Wounded Warrior Project: Veteran Peer Support Groups**

www.woundedwarriorproject.org · Resource Line for Learning about Support Groups: 888-997-2586 (888.WWP.ALUM)

Tackling the social isolation of veterans, the Wounded Warrior Project organizes veteran peer support groups for thirty-five states and is still growing. Groups offer peer led meetings and events across the country, including Alaska, Hawaii, Puerto Rico, and Guam. As a warrior, Carlos De Leon explained, "No one knows what you're going through better than someone who's been there." This organization brings the veteran community together for veterans to support one another. "Whether you're looking for someone to talk to or someone to spur you on to achieve your goals, Peer Support is here for you."

- **Village-to-Village Network (for people over fifty)**

www.vtvnetwork.org

The Village-to-Village Network (V-TV Network) is designed for people over fifty as a way to live in supportive communities that provide social support as we age. This membership-driven, grassroots, nonprofit organization is growing strongly throughout the US, and many area agencies on aging (AAA, www.n4a.org) can help with access to local V-TV networks. Hosting local social and community-building events, these "villages" are ideal support systems for seniors who may need to access transportation, medical providers, or other aging-related supports and resources.

- **Stitch (for people over fifty)**

www.stitch.net

This friendly, innovative, and fast-growing network is ideal for finding companionship and building community in person, and helps older adults team up for sharing their interests such as traveling, taking classes, socializing, dating, or just making new friends. Stitch networks are now in many states such as California, Nevada, Oregon, Florida, New York, Massachusetts, Iowa, Georgia, Illinois, and also sprouting in Costa Rica, Australia, England, and others. Local community organizers, called "community champions" serve as welcoming go-to people and contacts for new members.

- **Women Living in Community (over fifty)**

www.womenlivingincommunity.com

Founder Maryanne Kilkenny, author of *Your Quest for Home*, is a trailblazer in exploring alternative communities and shared housing opportunities for aging women. Her lively and helpful website is full of ideas, resources, and tips for finding house-sharing resources and contacts. Single women especially might find her site uplifting and useful.

- **Meetup.com**

Of course, meetups are everywhere and offer a wide assortment of groups, mostly for fun and sharing our interests. There are also groups for meeting people with similar, more serious (and isolating) issues. For example, if you struggle with social anxiety, there are now 1,062 social anxiety meetups around the world. But even if you are not anxious or shy, there is a meetup for everyone. Whether you identify as a foodie, an indie movie aficionada, a dog-lover, a birdwatcher, or just a nice geek, there is a meetup out there for you. (In Boston, there is even a meetup, "Regular Conversation Meetup," for those who just want to restore "regular conversation" by keeping their smartphones out of sight for at least an hour!)

And you can always create your own local meetup. If you happen to notice a meetup 3,000 miles across the country that looks perfect for you, you might contact their group organizers and pick their brains so you can get a new one started.

- **Common Sense Media**

www.commonsensemedia.org

This is a smart, helpful, and highly informative site to help family members and parents learn ways to manage technology with their children and teens. We can find guidance on how social media, video games, apps, and other devices are useful or harmful. It is full of fascinating research and advice on what is healthy or not for consumers of all ages. There are forums for discussion and interesting articles and news reports about the good, the bad, and the toxic uses of media.

- **The Clowder Group**

www.theclowdergroup.com

Joseph Applebaum and Stu Maddux are documentary filmmakers who are particularly concerned with social isolation and loneliness, and now in production with a feature-length film called *All the Lonely People* (www.allthelonelypeople.film) They are an award-winning team who created *Gen Silent*, a film about the loneliness and isolation of LGBTQ seniors.

- **SAGE Advocacy & Services for LGBT Elders**

www.sageusa.org · *SAGE Hotline: 877-360-LGBT*

LGBTQ seniors are twice as likely to live alone and more vulnerable to isolation. This nationwide organization provides training, advocacy, and support.

SUGGESTED READING

- **Belong: Find Your People, Create Community, and Live a More Connected Life**

  By Radha Agrawal. Workman Publishing, 2018.

  This is a hugely popular book that successfully serves as a helpful guide to building community, online and offline.

- **The Art of Gathering: How We Meet and Why It Matters**

  By Priya Parker. Riverhead Books, 2018.

  This book is full of enthusiasm, hope, and practical guidance on how to make our gatherings, both at work and at home, more meaningful and fulfilling.

- **With a Little Help from Our Friends: Creating Community as We Grow Older**

  By Beth Baker. Vanderbilt University Press, 2016.

  Written by a journalist who has interviewed many innovative leaders and founders, this much-needed guide is helpful, warm, and lively, devoted to people over fifty-five seeking to find or build supportive communities.

- **Loneliness: Human Nature and the Need for Social Connection**

  John Cacioppo and William Patrick. W.W. Norton, 2009.

  Social scientists from the University of Chicago present their findings after decades of research on loneliness and social isolation. This book is a must-read for anyone interested in a clinical understanding of how loneliness and isolation affects us as individuals—we are hardwired for human connection.

- **The Lonely American: Drifting Apart in the 21st Century**

Jacqueline Olds, MD, and Richard Schwartz, MD. Beacon Press, 2010.

The authors show us how fragile our human bonds can be in a world that prizes individuality, materialism, and ambition over community and connection.

- **Reclaiming Conversation: The Power of Talk in a Digital Age**

Sherry Turkle, PhD. Penguin/Random House, 2016.

As a social scientist and professor at MIT, Sherry Turkle brings thirty years of research into exploring how our digital age is limiting our ability to have conversations and shortchanging our deeper, more authentic connections. She offers eye-opening examples of how conversation is disappearing when smartphones are in use and even when they are in view. She makes a compelling case for preserving and protecting our offscreen time for healthier connections.

- **iGen: Why Today's Super-Connected Kids Are Growing Up Less Rebellious, More Tolerant, Less Happy— and Completely Unprepared for Adulthood— and What That Means for the Rest of Us**

Jean M. Twenge, PhD. Atria Books, 2017.

Dr. Twenge, a professor at San Diego State University, explores how heavy social media use affects teens and young adults. This book can be a game-changer for teachers, parents, counselors, and others working with this population to understand how anxious and hypervigilant we have become as a culture by constantly comparing ourselves with others. This book shows us why so many young people avoid casual conversation and offscreen connections.

- **Social: Why Our Brains Are Wired to Connect**

Matthew D. Lieberman. Broadway Books, 2014.

A psychologist explores groundbreaking research in social neuroscience. For a clinical grasp of how our brains work to build connections and learn from one another, this books clearly tells us the latest finds with what MRI scans (magnetic resonance imaging scans) are showing us. We are even hardwired for softness—to harness our empathy and to share it.

- **There Is No Good Card for This:**
What to Say and Do When Life Is Scary,
Awful, and Unfair to Those You Love

Kelsey Crowe, PhD, and Emily McDowell. HarperOne, 2017.

The creator of Empathy Cards teamed up with a social work professor at California State University to create a lively, friendly, and helpful guide to reaching out to people at difficult times. I recommend this book for learning the skills for reaching out—how to offer our care and comfort to people in isolating times. Their tips can help those of us who feel isolated reach out to others in awkward or delicate situations and make meaningful connections.

- **The Art of Comforting: What to Say and Do for People in Distress**

Val Walker. Penguin/Random House, 2010.

My first book explores how to be a comforting presence for people facing grief, illness, trauma, and other losses. We learn the language of empathy for putting compassion into action with others during lonely and distressing times. It won the Nautilus Book Award in 2011 and was recommended by the Boston Public Health Commission as a guide for families involved with the Boston Marathon Bombing.

- **24/6: The Power of Unplugging One Day a Week**

Tiffany Shlain. Gallery Books, 2019.

A much-needed, easy-to-read, yet realistic guidebook to encourage us to get off our screens for the sake of our relationships.

- **Cut Adrift: Families in Insecure Times**

Marianne Cooper, PhD. University of California Press, 2014.

If any writer can examine the pitfalls of living in survival mode for struggling American families, Dr. Cooper does this brilliantly. With eye-opening social science research, her book shows us how socio-economic factors isolate us and cause painful barriers to opportunities for healthy human connections.

WEBSITES OF CONTRIBUTORS

- **Annie Brewster, MD:**

  Health Story Collaborative and The Opioid Project

  www.healthstorycollaborative.org

  The Opioid Project

  https://opioidproject.oncell.com

- **Allie Cashel:**

  Suffering the Silence

  www.sufferingthesilence.com

- **Marisa Renee Lee:**

  Supportal

  www.meetsupportal.com

- **Ana Bess Moyer Bell:**

  COAAST (Creating Outreach About Addiction Support Together)

  www.coaast.org

- **Robyn Houston-Bean:**

  The Sun Will Rise Foundation

  www.thesunwillrise.org

- **Sharon Perfetti:**

  Paul Partnership

  www.paulpartnership.com

- **Claus Adam Jarlov:**

  Global Denmark

  https://global-denmark.dk

Acknowledgments

Writers typically need to shut themselves off in a quiet, contained space for hours, days, or weeks at a time to focus. I can absolutely testify to this sacred practice of unplugging from everyone and all distractions while I work. And I love it! Creating a book, let alone an article, requires my utmost devotion, and I'm usually fulfilled by the whole process, from thinking deeply for hours by my window, jotting down notes in a journal, to gathering research, to final edits.

But this sweet immersion and devotion to my art comes at a high price. I must admit that serious writing can be highly isolating at times. Thus, as the author of a book about social isolation and loneliness, I declare a great irony: In my determination to finish these 250 pages, and in my rush to meet my publisher's deadlines, I isolated myself from my loved ones and friends to get the job done. God bless them all—I'm *still* promising, month after month, that I will "resurface" soon and visit them, but I have not kept these promises. On the few, precious occasions when I have met with them, I have tried to weave into their lives some threads of discovery and healing that writing this book has given me. Thankfully, fortunately, most people have appreciated (or even been inspired by) the revelations I've made by exploring the deepest, most stigmatized and shameful aspects of social isolation. I've had extraordinarily meaningful conversations with loved ones on this provocative topic.

The first friend with whom I shared my dream of writing my book was Amy Handy back in 2016. I lived with her for two months, between my many moves, trying to find affordable housing. In exchange for letting me stay with her for a very small rent, I cooked dinners for her, and afterword we lingered at the table for hours. Her father had just died, her daughters were off on their own, and her husband, a flight attendant, was often away in other cities, so Amy had her own isolation to talk about. It was suddenly clear to me that she felt just as isolated as I did. Her loneliness and sense of disconnection was not just a thing that single, older, childless women like me suffered—it was universal. Isolation could strike us suddenly or creep up on us, no matter whether we had "support systems" or not. Our long conversations sparked new chapters in my book, and one year later, Amy, who happens to be a freelance editor, was reviewing and editing my work. We made a good team. She trusted me well enough to get me to tone down my bitter laments about the abandonment of my friends, employers, doctors, mates, or colleagues. She encouraged me to find the right balance between pity party whining and telling a good story. It was, quite frankly, a mutually healing experience, as she also took her own advice with reframing her own misfortunes. Good stories come out of bad stuff, that is, if we tell it the right way. (Not at all an original thought, I know. But mercifully true.)

Once Amy and I got the book going, much fell into place after that. I want to give a shout out to my agent, Peter Rubie, at FinePrint Literary Management, who believed in my book proposal and shopped it around until Valerie Killeen, the acquisitions editor at Central Recovery Press, enthusiastically discovered it. I am deeply grateful for their connection in December of 2018—a Christmas present of sorts. I offer whole-hearted thanks to the team at Central Recovery Press, editing with Nancy Schenk, and book promotion with Patrick Hughes and Kelli Daniel. I am also happy to add that Central Recovery Press helped to finance video production and other marketing and speaking initiatives—so generously supportive.

The fifteen contributors who bravely and creatively allowed me to profile them and shared their own stories so candidly and generously—I will never be able to thank them enough! Once again, please give a shout out to Paul and his son, Paul, Ana Bess, Robyn, Annie, Marisa, Allie, Sharon, Karen, Morna, Lee, Ben, Pam, Claus, and Jan! It would have been a sad, boring book without them all chiming in with my long saga through isolating times and back out again.

Alongside my team at Central Recovery Press, and in addition to my book's contributors, I had many others rooting for my book to get out into the world. Barbara Olson, my first friend in Boston, who is a professional photographer, offered to do a photo shoot that produced a lovely headshot of me for my book. I am also touched by the generosity of other dear friends who allowed me to share their stories in my book, although I changed their names and specific information to protect their identities. I appreciate the hopes and wishes of my father and sister, Maguire, two highly creative people who believed in my arduous path of being serious with my writing. I also treasure the other writers and artists around me who have inspired me, especially when they've made huge personal and financial sacrifices to start and grow their projects and enterprises. It takes great courage and vision to take action, and a certain amount of superhuman energy after the age of sixty. Life gets a hell of a lot more complicated when your project is in development and so much else must take the back burner. You keep praying things don't boil over on those back burners so you can, God help you, keep up the intense focus and get it done.

Blessed with a loving group of friends and my sister, Kim, and her sweetheart, Bob, who helped me after my surgery while finishing my manuscript, I'm certain I'm well-supported and not isolated anymore. The person who started writing this book in 2013 is not the same person who is writing these acknowledgment pages today. My book chronicles my six-year journey out of isolation, and I now hold in my heart the warmth of gratitude and a quiet, steady sense of belonging.

It just doesn't get much sweeter than this: I wrote the book I couldn't find about my sense of isolation, and I discovered that my community had been there all along.